# ALIGN YOUR
# BUSINESS
### ═══ with the ═══
# REAL YOU

# ALIGN YOUR BUSINESS
=== with the ===
# REAL YOU

CONNECT WITH YOURSELF,
CREATE WHAT MATTERS MOST,
AND DEFINE YOUR SUCCESS

## Jennifer Musser

PenRock
-press-

*Align Your Business with the Real You:*
*Connect with Yourself, Create What Matters Most, and Define Your Success*
Copyright © 2025, Jennifer Musser. All rights reserved, including the right to reproduce this book or portions thereof in any form whatsoever. No claim to the trademarks of others is made.

No AI Training: Without in any way limiting the author's exclusive rights under copyright, any use of this publication to "train" generative artificial intelligence (AI) technologies is expressly prohibited. The author reserves all rights to license uses of this work for generative AI training and development of machine learning language models including AI technologies and tools to create publications or other products or services using this work.

Published in the United States by PenRock press, West Caldwell, New Jersey.

PenRock press, LTY, ALD, and The Gratitude Equation are trademarks of JLM & Associates Consulting, LLC.

JLMAConsulting.com

For information about special discounts for bulk purchases, please contact Marketing@JLMAConsulting.com.

Without limiting the rights under copyright reserved above, no part of this publication may be reproduced, stored in or introduced into an algorithm, model or tool, including virtual, cloud or other retrieval system, or transmitted in any form or by any means (digital, electronic, mechanical, photocopying, recording, or otherwise, whether now or hereafter known), without the prior written permission of both the copyright owner and the above publisher of this book, except by a reviewer who wishes to quote brief passages in connection with a review written for insertion in a magazine, newspaper, broadcast, website, blog, or other outlet in conformity with United States and International Fair Use or comparable guidelines to such copyright exceptions.

This book is intended to provide accurate information with regard to its subject matter and reflects the opinion and perspective of the author. However, in times of rapid change, ensuring all information provided is entirely accurate and up-to-date at all times is not always possible. Therefore, the author and publisher undertake no obligation to update any information in this book and accept no responsibility for inaccuracies or omissions and specifically disclaim any liability, loss, or risk, personal, professional, or otherwise, which may be incurred as a consequence, directly or indirectly, of the use and/or application of any of the contents of this book.

Publication managed by AuthorImprints.com
Cover design by Hannah Linder
Author photographs by Susie Mann

ISBN 979-8-9915442-1-4 (paperback)
ISBN 979-8-9915442-2-1 (hardcover)
ISBN 979-8-9915442-0-7 (eBook)
Library of Congress Control Number: 2024921354

Publisher's Cataloging-in-Publication
(Provided by Cassidy Cataloguing Services, Inc.)
| | |
|---|---|
| Names: | Musser, Jennifer, author. |
| Title: | Align your business with the real you : connect with yourself, create what matters most, and define your success / Jennifer Musser. |
| Description: | West Caldwell, New Jersey : PenRock press, [2025] |
| Identifiers: | ISBN: 979-8-9915442-1-4 (paperback) | 979-8-9915442-2-1 (hardcover) | 979-8-9915442-0-7 (ebook) | LCCN: 2024921354 |
| Subjects: | LCSH: Success in business. | Businesspeople. | Small business. | Management. | Time management. | Work-life balance. | BISAC: BUSINESS & ECONOMICS / Small Business. | BUSINESS & ECONOMICS / Skills. | BUSINESS & ECONOMICS / Time Management. |
| Classification: | LCC: HF5386 .M87 2025 | DDC: 650.1--dc23 |

*For my amazing husband Mark, our precious son Richard, our beloved dog Roxy, who was eighteen when I started manifesting this book, and our two special pups, Penny and Rockie, who found us and each other.*

*We built a beautiful life together. Richard, any dream of yours is achievable. I love you all forever and ever.*

# CONTENTS

Introduction    A Founder Chooses What They Find    1

## Part One
## Connect: Listen to Yourself    9
Chapter 1    Find Where You Belong    11
Chapter 2    Conquer Opportunities    23

## Part Two
## Clarify: Understand Your Role in Your Journey    37
Chapter 3    Optimize Your Performance    39
Chapter 4    Focus to Win    53

## Part Three
## Control: Take Charge of Your Life    69
Chapter 5    Carve Out Space    71
Chapter 6    Learn to Chill    87
Chapter 7    Look Inside    103

**Part Four**
**Cocreate: Create What Matters Most**     **117**

Chapter 8    Feel Your Emotions     119
Chapter 9    Shift Your Perspective     137
Chapter 10    Renew Your Energy     155

**Part Five**
**Change: Transform Your Experience**     **171**

Chapter 11    Be Your Catalyst for Change     173
Chapter 12    Stop Trying to Do It All     189
Chapter 13    Appreciate the Real You     203

Conclusion    A Founder Chooses What Success Means     219

**Further Resources**     **223**
**Discussion Guide**     **225**
**Workbook Exercises**     **231**
**Acknowledgments and Gratitude**     **259**
**About the Author**     **263**

## INTRODUCTION
# A FOUNDER CHOOSES WHAT THEY FIND

Dear Courageous, Curious, and Creative Fellow Founders,

As you know, owning a company can be all-consuming.

You have taken a courageous leap of faith to pursue your entrepreneurial endeavors. You wake up happy, knowing you love what you do. However, you also wake up tired. Worries about productivity, risk, or money distract you from living in the present. You laugh, smile, and enjoy your work. You also feel stressed, unfocused, worried, confused, or disconnected. Depending on the day, you may feel all those emotions.

The days of the week blur together. There just don't seem to be enough hours in the day to check off what you need to do for work, family, and yourself. At night, you lay in bed with creative ideas swirling in your mind. As you stare at the ceiling, you feel like you are wasting time and sleep. You are maxed out.

You spend your best energy each day helping your customers see and solve their problems. Meanwhile, you may be wondering how well you're recognizing and solving your own. Regardless of age, gender, geography, industry, or business longevity, as founders, we share certain challenges and uncertainties. No one has it all figured out. Even the most qualified, experienced, and confident business professionals do not have all the answers all the time. There's no golden key to an easy, smooth entrepreneurial life. In the life of a founder, there are bumps in the road, doubt in the mind, and plentiful lessons to unveil.

Do any of the following questions sound familiar?

*How do I stay focused in the daily bustle of my life?*
*How do I feel fulfilled while supporting significant others, employees, clients, employers, supervisors, community—even kids, aging parents, and pets?*
*How do I gain traction to move forward, feeling less confused, conflicted, and frustrated?*
*How do I give myself the support I need?*
*How do I connect with others who lift me up rather than those who zap my energy?*
*How do I feel a sense of bliss in my life in all its areas: my inner circle, business, relationships, and community?*
*And how do I get a good night's sleep?*

> **There is a path forward to define your success.**

As entrepreneurs, we want to know how. No surprise. We are curious types.

It's okay to feel a disconnect between what you want and how to dissect it. It's okay to want a more fulfilling life but have no idea how you're going to achieve it. It's okay to wonder who truly belongs in your inner circle. It's okay to feel like the line between your business and personal lives is blurred—or nonexistent. It's okay to have answers for your customers more than for yourself right now. It's all okay.

There is a path forward to define your success.

A "before" entrepreneurship story resides in each of us. For me, I began my career in big business. I was fortunate to have some career opportunities that stretched me like Gumby. Since I possessed mental horsepower coupled with a desire to excel, I kept growing more and more.

My global consulting career commenced in New York City. As a result, I had the opportunity to travel internationally, which helped shape the person I am today, including my love of fashion (and shoes). During this time, I led multiple engagement teams performing pre- and post-merger and acquisition business and asset valuations worldwide for private and publicly held companies. I also helped build a New York City valuation practice, which required entrepreneurial skills and a deep and broad understanding of business intricacies. I had to see the big picture, execute daily operations, and provide stellar client service.

Eventually, I was curious about working in the corporate world rather than bouncing from client to client. So I became a finance and accounting head, building, analyzing, and reporting strategic plans, budgets, forecasts, and key performance indicators rather than serving as the consultant reviewing them.

I was intrigued and invigorated by turnaround and restructuring work, which fueled me for a time. I learned how to be a strategic CFO. I learned how to work for an intense CEO with a solid track record. I learned a lot about a lot.

However, I wanted and needed more in some areas and less in others. At times, I felt confined, conflicted, overlooked, overutilized, undervalued, undermined, dimmed, discouraged, depleted, and well, lost in it all. Like you, I also had needs, desires, and realistic dreams.

Fast-forward to my entrepreneurial journey. I poured all the knowledge, experience, and strength I amassed, including the plentiful internal struggles, into founding my business. Meanwhile, I hadn't fully sorted through my treasure chest of courage, wisdom, or serenity.

One Monday morning, I was on my fourth cup of black coffee before 7:30, and I wasn't feeling the slightest jolt of energy or inspiration. I'm the go, go, go type. However, whether you told me it was Saturday or Tuesday, I wouldn't have known the difference. Within two years of starting my consulting business, I was facing the reality that the life of a founder was exciting but exhausting.

I knew in my heart it didn't have to feel this way. I didn't need to "fix" anything. I didn't need a vacation, spa day, or bubble bath. At times, I just needed to feel my emotions. I also needed to look at my life from a fresh perspective. So I started asking myself questions like, *Why do I feel so disconnected from myself? Why do things seem so unclear? Why does my life as a business owner feel all-consuming?*

After taking a deep breath (I do that a lot now), I assembled guidelines about what I knew to be true to me:

- I *value* my health, time, freedom, family, and friends.
- I *want* a successful career with a sense of freedom that makes my business pursuits and sacrifices worthwhile.
- I *desire* change to give me more time and energy to focus on my business (not just work in my business) and on what I value most.
- I *need* to take a deep breath, reduce stress, and ease my restlessness.
- I *can* trust myself more.
- I *am* the leader of *all* aspects of my life.

These ideas led me to a question that changed everything:
*Who's really running my business, anyway?*
At the time, I felt like my business and its insatiable task list were ruling my world. I had sucked myself into trying to do too much. I was also honing my communication skills to convey my big-business experience and key strengths, plus the fact that I lead with genuine kindness. One of my most frustrating challenges was that kind, upbeat, and personable was sometimes perceived as pliable, inexperienced, and naive.

I stopped, breathed, and reassessed. I realized that the answer to "Who's really running my business?" is me. The *real me*.

The real me envisioned doing meaningful work with kind, genuine, open-minded clients, colleagues, and connections. The real me was the person who asks you how you are—and actually listens to and cares about your answer. The real me had unwavering resilience in the face of criticism. This was who I wanted to project into my new entrepreneurial world. From that day forward, the real me chose how I wanted to show up and where.

That's when I chose a life more aligned with the real me. No more what-ifs or shoulds. No more looking outside of myself for validation or listening to others steer me toward no, wait, or why. I realized that everything I needed to connect with myself and others was within me. *It's within you too.*

My inner turmoil—from cancer to motherhood to personal loss to layoff—unveiled the lessons I needed to digest, learn, and apply. I am grateful to be here to share those with you now.

My journey through this unveiling, taking leap after leap into the unknown, did not come easily. More on that unfolds in the pages of this book. In the meantime, here's the shortcut.

*A founder chooses what they find.*

As a business owner, you are in full control of your journey, including your perspective (and your insatiable task lists). There's always more to learn, so there is no finish line and nowhere to "arrive."

Are you ready to take control of your business and align it with the real you?

If you are, I believe we are meant to be on a path together. I'm here to help guide you with strategic purpose toward your own successful outcomes, with less stress and restlessness. I'm here to help you help yourself.

Together, we will navigate things we all experience as founders but rarely make the time to think about or solve. I will steer you without giving you the answers or telling you what to do. I vow to avoid reciting research, studies, or statistics. You have all the research you need through your individual experiences. You are in charge of yourself, your business, and your life.

So think of me as your purposeful guide, connecting and conversing with you while empowering you with actionable insights and practical advice based on my real and sometimes messy journey. I did not employ AI or a ghostwriter. This is the real me uniting in purpose with the real you.

## ALIGN YOUR BUSINESS WITH THE REAL YOU

*Align Your Business with the Real You* is designed to give you a five-step process, with practical lessons and key takeaways, to propel you forward wherever you are on your entrepreneurship journey. My 5C framework is based on my years of career and life experiences:

1. **Connect:** Listen to yourself.
2. **Clarify:** Understand your role in your journey.
3. **Control:** Take charge of your life.
4. **Cocreate:** Construct the life you envision for yourself and with others.
5. **Change:** Transform your experience.

Throughout the 5Cs, you will find thirteen practical lessons. You will discover these thirteen diamonds one at a time. The title of each chapter gives you a hint, it's the mental shift to make to discover the lesson.

Each chapter follows the pattern of the natural way life lessons are accumulated: experience, reflect, learn, apply, act, and ask (reflect). At the beginning of each chapter, I recount a personal event to explain how my experience shaped the end realization. Because the 5Cs follow a sequential order, my flashbacks are embedded for relevance rather than sequence. Think of the flashbacks as less about me and more about you; parts of my story are communicated to illustrate how I navigated circumstances, gathered awakening moments, and reached the point where I can help guide you through a similar situation.

Let my pain points become your gain. These are insights that took me two decades to figure out, and I'm sharing them to help you emerge as the calmer, confident, and gratified business owner you are more than capable of becoming. At the end of each chapter, I provide an exercise and reflection questions for you to integrate the lesson in your life over the long term.

More than simply reading this book, I want you to use it and reuse it. Some readers will enjoy completing exercises as they go; others will prefer to read the entire book to get the big picture and return to the exercises later. That's why, at the end of this book, you'll find a discussion guide with all the reflection questions gathered in one place, in case you'd like to take additional time to reflect with yourself, your inner circle, other business owners, or a book club. You'll also find a mini workbook that contains all the chapter exercises if you prefer to put the lessons into practice later. This book is intended to be a resource you can refer back to as many times as you desire.

Now, take a deep breath. You've got this. Join me on a leadership journey through which you will learn to trust yourself more. Bring along *kindness* because it *can flow* through your business *as a strength* (more on that later).

You *can* run your business and your life in a way that alleviates some of the angst, confusion, and frustration of business ownership. It all starts with the first of my 5Cs.

You are a talented business owner ready to make *your* success about the *real* you. That's why you're here. I'm here to support you in finding what you choose to find on this journey, as the clouds part, the sun shines, and you emerge in your true magnificence.

Best wishes for a bright, enduring future for the real you and your business,

*Jennifer*

# PART ONE
# CONNECT: LISTEN TO YOURSELF

Do you feel connected with yourself? Do you feel in sync with your business and your life?

Your ability to connect with yourself and others is an asset, and the most valuable connection you can make is with yourself. It is never too late to connect with yourself. In Chapter 1, you'll learn how connecting with yourself allows you to find where you belong in life and business. In Chapter 2, you'll discover how knowing where you belong positions you to connect with like-minded others and conquer the right opportunities. As worthwhile experiences flow, the clouds begin to part. You feel engaged *and* at peace.

Let's connect.

## CHAPTER 1
# FIND WHERE YOU BELONG

Have you ever walked into a room or gathering and knew you were in the right place at the right time?

As I scribbled notes and formulas during a dreaded chemistry class, my mind wandered. Although I was physically present, the rest of me was contemplating what I wanted to do with my life. I remember looking around the lecture hall that day, wondering if anyone felt like me.

I felt confused by feelings of disconnection, distraction, and defeat. I had already spent about half a semester waffling: Do I plug along unhappily to follow my childhood dream, or do I give up on that dream and switch to a major I could enjoy?

Up to that point, my heart had been set on becoming a veterinarian. I loved animals, and I had dogs throughout my entire life (currently, I have two). As a child, one of my favorite toys was the doctor kit my parents gave me, which I used to "play vet" with Max, our fluffy, seventy-pound black-and-white English setter. Plus, math and science were my favorite subjects.

By my junior year in high school, my heart was also set on attending Villanova University. I don't know why, exactly, none of my family members or friends had attended Villanova. I liked the not-too-big, not-too-small, attractive suburban campus with stone buildings close to Philadelphia, its academic offerings, and the community vibe. I was intent on spending four years of my life there, complete with living on the "quad" during my sophomore year. My end goal was establishing my own veterinary practice.

When I was accepted into Villanova as a biology major, I was ecstatic.

Then I was conflicted.

Thoughts of "failing" and "quitting" swirled around my young mind. I was tormenting myself with scenarios involving maybes, what-ifs, and shoulds. I didn't want to "give up." I thought I could conquer chemistry. If I let my dream go, I would feel like advanced chemistry defeated me in some way.

Despite my determination and extra studying, the complicated chemistry formulas weren't clicking. The more I focused, the worse it seemed to get, which added more frustration to the mix. I felt drained.

As I sat there, writing down chemistry formulas, I knew this would be one of the last chemistry classes I'd ever sit through. That realization yielded a cocktail of emotion: two parts relief, one part disappointment.

My inner voice was telling me that if I wanted to be true to myself, it was time to move in a different direction. Not only that, but I had to figure out how to transfer from one track to another as quickly as possible.

Later that week, my connection to myself brought me to Bartley Hall and the Villanova School of Business. When you find where you belong, you feel it. Opening the heavy door to Bartley Hall unveiled a new world. Within seconds, a relaxed sense of clarity comforted me.

The atmosphere felt inviting. The air even smelled different from West Campus. More windows let more light in. The upperclassmen, who didn't even know me, offered welcoming glances and hellos. Overall, there was a different sort of hustle to the bustle. I was meeting my soon-to-be business school advisor. We had already talked on the phone, so I felt at ease as I walked into his office. We exchanged broad smiles. Our conversation flowed naturally. He asked meaningful questions and listened intently to the answers. We chatted about my academic interests, personal development pursuits, career goals, volunteer activities, and some family stuff.

Then we mapped out an academic plan for the next semester and beyond. He even recommended getting involved quickly in business-related extracurriculars, like the Financial Management Association (encouraging me to become president by my senior year). Although I had some heavy coursework lifting to do, he helped me see through some thick clouds of confusion and painted a big picture where nothing was out of reach if I wanted to reach it.

I was struck by his kindness. That one meeting shaped my future career, which impacted my life in a huge way.

By the time I left Bartley Hall that day, I had committed to switch my major from biology to finance. I didn't quit or fail. I simply changed academic homes within the same university. In doing so, I felt uplifted, more confident, and more connected with myself.

At eighteen, I had discovered what it meant to connect with myself—and to "pivot."

## Reflect

Although I didn't know where the journey would lead, one door after another opened, and it all began with my choice to connect with myself. My inner knowing steered me toward facing my reality to figure out what career path was best suited for me.

Looking back now, it's easy to see that my uncertainty surrounding what I wanted to do for the rest of my life was okay and even expected at such a young age. I had to rely on my inner guidance and strength to learn this life lesson.

**Change course when a new path feels right.**

Why is this story from my college days relevant now? Because the lesson I learned had a profound impact on my life. It served me well in many situations for decades to come. It can serve you well too.

Sometimes you go into a situation or phase of life sure about how it will turn out. Then things unfold differently than planned or desired. If you're continuing to evolve throughout your life, you encounter many critical moments that affect your career trajectory.

Whether you're on a college campus, in the C-suite, or at your home office, what matters is doing what it takes to find where you belong. This takes courage, strength, and heart.

This is the first lesson because it affects everything else you do. In life and especially in business, the only constant is change. The need to pivot doesn't evaporate when you reach a certain age or stage. Aligning your business with the real you begins with connecting with yourself, taking control of your journey, and changing course when necessary.

## Learn

What does it mean to "find where you belong" in your career? Belonging isn't about external characteristics, like degrees or grades or popularity or status. It's about internally sensing when your purpose, goals, relationships, and well-being *align*. It's about feeling connected with yourself, others, and your environment.

How do you know if you're *not* where you belong? Here are some questions to consider:

- Do you feel confused?
- Is your confusion leading to frustration?
- Is your frustration leading to inaction?
- Is your inaction causing feelings of disconnection from yourself or your business?

If you answered yes to the questions above, these symptoms may indicate it's time to pivot. Remember, confusion alone is not a sign you need to pivot. Life is confusing. Owning a business can make it even more so. As you can see from the questions above, I'm talking about the type of confusion that consistently leaves you debilitated, stuck, drained, or so buried in your thoughts or fears or doubts that you're *thinking* more than you're *doing*. We will dedicate more time to thinking versus acting in Chapter 10. For now, recognize that spending too much time in your head can cause you to disconnect from yourself and others. If overthinking is an ongoing pattern for you, it might be a sign you're staying put when you could be moving on.

On the other hand, perhaps even the thought of changing course triggers more confusion, frustration, and disconnection. *What if I fail? What if I lose time? What if I lose money? What if I don't succeed?* If you've invested years or even decades in your current career path, change may feel too risky.

> **Alignment unleashes your highest level of productivity and contribution in this world.**

The reality is it can be riskier *not* to change course if you are no longer in alignment with your current path. As a business owner, consider the following risks related to your *time*, *connections*, and *outcomes*, which are all intertwined:

- **Time:** Intellectually, you know time is finite. The longer you spend on a path that's not for you, the less time you will have on the one that is, or to pave your own.
- **Connections:** Connecting with yourself and others is so critical because those connections impact your life experiences—both present and future. If you are on the most suitable path for you, you can link with like-minded folks. Once you get onboard the right train, you are sitting with those invested in reaching the same destination, which expands your opportunities far beyond what you could achieve on your own. Or, to use another metaphor, you can't bring your A game when you're not on the right field.
- **Outcomes:** When you're where you belong, your impact increases exponentially. For example, when you enjoy what you're doing, you're energized, so the quality of your work improves. Also, challenges become exciting rather than burdensome, so you willingly take on

more of them. When you take on more challenges while producing higher-quality work, you receive more opportunities to succeed at a higher level. And when you succeed at a higher level, you can impact more people while also having more resources to invest in the projects and relationships that matter most to you.

Sure, you can get by in any environment. But alignment unleashes your highest level of productivity and contribution in this world. Which do you choose?

The good news is that pivoting may be less risky than you think. You can find where you belong without leaving where you are. I discovered my new career path without changing my college address. It is possible to change course and restore alignment without having to start over.

If you're a business owner, you already embarked on an entrepreneurial journey to get to where you are right now. Changing direction can transpire within your existing business, within your current industry. For example, you might alter your network to connect with others more interested in supporting you and your business, or you might approach a different audience more in need of what you offer. A more drastic change might be closing one business and starting a new one that becomes even more successful because it aligns with your strengths, passions, and personality—as well as your financial resources and risk tolerance.

Remember, opportunities to pivot will happen throughout your life, whether you are twenty, forty, sixty, or beyond. Age is irrelevant. What is relevant is your current path, which affects your future opportunities, accomplishments, connections, outcomes, and spirit. If you realize the path you're on is not in alignment with who you are at this time in your life, changing course is not quitting. It's simply redirecting yourself to where you need to go.

## Apply

Of course, redirecting yourself is easier said than done. Whether in a personal or professional context, changing course requires resilience and flexibility.

Here are some practical steps for knowing when and how to pivot:

1. **Recognize when something doesn't feel right.** If something doesn't feel right, it doesn't mean you are lost or failing. It simply means something feels off-kilter. If so, you are normal, and you're not alone. You also don't need to know what to do about it immediately. For example, I knew something was amiss when I didn't sync with organic chemistry. I detected it wasn't just the class; the whole environment of my major wasn't fulfilling me, either. The more I tried to suck it up, the more stifling my lab coat felt.

Okay, something doesn't feel right. Now what?

2. **Connect with yourself.** When it comes to finding where you belong, no guru or expert can give you the answers. Nobody can tell you where you belong except you. That means, as the leader of your life, you need to connect with the true expert in this situation: *you*.

    How do you connect with yourself? Yoga headstands or meditation retreats aren't required. All that's required is the ability to identify what makes you feel more engaged, stimulated, and, well, happy.

    Simply spend a few minutes with yourself. Remove the background noise and listen to the channel of your mind. Do you feel confused? Do you feel frustrated because you don't know what to do next? Do you feel like you're doing work that suits you?

    In some cases, the most useful knowledge to apply to your life is what you learn about yourself. For me, as I became aware of new career options, I realized the business world appealed to me more than the sciences.

    I got curious about why. So I asked myself these questions:

What was missing from my experience?
*More group interaction and levity.*
What subject matter did I like the least?
*Chemistry.*
Did I enjoy working in groups or individually?
*Both.*
Did I like working with numbers?
*Yes.*
Where did I want to work?
*New York City.*

As a result of connecting with myself, I began to see how business might be the missing piece in the puzzle. Solving chemistry problems didn't feel right because I was meant to use my math and logic skills to solve business problems in a different work environment.

Again, no one gave me this list of questions or told me I belonged in undergraduate business school. I needed to solve my own problem by asking my own questions. By connecting with yourself, you can too.

3. **Connect with others aligned with your new path**. After you do the work of connecting with yourself, identifying, and connecting with those who can support you on your new path flows naturally.

   Once I connected with what I truly enjoyed enough to formulate a sensible new direction, I reached out to connect with others who could guide me. The door to Bartley Hall opened at my choosing after I had connected with myself first. I gelled with my advisor in the business school because I was craving fresh ideas, ready to listen, and willing to change paths. As a result, my readiness set the tone for our meeting, which then unveiled a whole new world of opportunities.

   At the same time, my advisor's warm welcoming smile was genuine; he truly wanted me to succeed in finance. You need folks like that on your success team. He was the right coach for me at the right time. In turn, I was motivated to bring my best self to his classes, projects, and extracurriculars.

Actively adjust your network to connect with like-minded people who want to support you in your new direction (and who you want to support as well). It no longer makes sense to nurture one-sided relationships or spend time with those who don't have your best interests in mind. The quality of your relationships influences your outcomes.

Get out of your comfort zone to mingle. It doesn't require a huge time investment; you can easily set aside even one hour a month or one event per quarter to start. Try different networking events. Go to reputable conferences within your industry. Sign up for virtual sessions. Tap into LinkedIn. There is something for every business owner. Some you will like; some you won't. The ones you do enjoy can be found in environments in which you can thrive. Think of this as self-care time for your business. Make it happen.

So where are you now? Are you where you belong?

- Have you realized your work life is good enough as is and you don't need to change a thing?
- Are you on the right track for your business and have some tweaks to make?
- Do you need to change paths within the same market, perhaps with respect to your target audience or your connections?
- Or do you need to make a *big* change? If so, is your mind saying, *I don't have time for this. I don't even know where to start?*

Now what? Take a breath.

Even if you need to make a big change, you can start with one small change. Little adjustments lead to huge strides.

Wherever you find yourself, *commit to act* with intention and speed. Business owners need to make decisions without waffling. Rash, impulsive, or uninformed decisions are not recommended. The speed of your strategic decisions drives execution, saving you time and angst in the long run.

## Act: Then, Now, Next

Here is an exercise to try as your next step. (Remember, all the exercises also appear at the end of the book for your convenience. If you'd prefer to keep reading and complete the exercises later, please do. This book was designed to offer you flexibility, so use it to your advantage.)

If you think you might need to change course, consider the following questions:

1. **Then:** Think back to recall how many times you have pivoted since the "green" phase of your early twenties. How did you know you needed to make a change? Any answer is a good one here, as it will help you recognize similar circumstances now.
2. **Now:** Shift your focus to your current situation. In your current work life, what makes you whirl in circles? We're not talking about tasks you'd rather not deal with, like bookkeeping or tax planning (we'll deal with delegation later); think of situations where you feel as if you're unable to move forward. We're often trying to avoid some inner discomfort, or we don't have the strategic expertise to know how to move forward. In either case, we don't resolve the issue.
3. **Next:** Now that you've uncovered what makes you swirl, how do you stop it? Remember your commitment to act with intention and strategic speed. Use what you know about yourself and your business to get on the most suitable success path. For example, if marketing to your target audience is falling flat, it's time to adjust. If your business model is the source of your angst, lead yourself to the root cause. Be honest with yourself.

    If you can't solve it alone, tap into your connections to seek advice or hire expert guidance within your budget. Chapter 12 dives further into this topic. For now, keep in mind that the longer you delay, the more you are exacerbating your business issue.

*Remember, changing course is an opportunity to elevate your experience.*

## Ask

1. Think of a time when you had to make a profound pivot. How did you recognize that a change in course would suit you better? How did you feel before, during, and after this pivot?
2. What does "find where you belong" mean to you in the context of your career and life?

## SOLIDIFY WHAT YOU'VE LEARNED

◊ **LESSON 1:** Change course when a new path feels right.

## CHAPTER 2
# CONQUER OPPORTUNITIES

Have you ever found yourself someplace completely unexpected and needed to learn a new way of living or working?

Basel. Leeds. London. Paris. Zurich.

In my role at a global consulting firm, routine international travel was expected. My suitcase was always packed with necessities, ready to roll. However, this suitcase hadn't ventured to Asia. Until now.

As the plane ascended through the clouds toward Tokyo, visions of what the next few high-pressured days could be like raced through my mind. I spent most of the fourteen-hour plane ride thinking about how this trip would unfold, pondering questions like, *How would we be perceived? Would we show respect correctly? Would the clients be welcoming? Did I pack the right clothes?* I opened the book I purchased for the occasion to review essential cultural etiquette once again. *Remember the three different levels of bowing. No eye contact while bowing. Remove shoes upon entering buildings.* Feeling mentally prepared, I fell asleep and woke up in Tokyo.

The client was indeed welcoming, sending a spotless, polished black Mercedes sedan and impeccably groomed driver to transport us to the hotel. The driver and I exchanged bows and faint smiles. The car ride offered glimpses of the city alive with swarms of pedestrians walking the streets like most other major cities. The top-rated hotel was gorgeous and super clean, with cordial customer service. After testing out the subtle bowing motion as a polite and humble gesture, I felt more at ease in this faraway city. The first client meeting would be the real test.

Fueled with coffee and purpose, I was ready. The purpose was to value the assets of a company merging with our large, global-industry-leading, publicly traded client. This strategic alliance required an asset valuation to be performed swiftly, with excellence.

Upon arriving at the client's office, we were greeted pleasantly by the entire team. Relief number one. The bows exchanged were the second type of bowing I read about—not too formal, not too casual. Relief number two. Poised in my favorite suit and fashionable black Manolo Blahniks, I followed their lead. Next came the shoe removal before entering the large conference room. As I added my shoes to the lineup, three thoughts popped into my head: the clients sported high-end shoes, my heels were the only female ones in the lot, and I was glad I brought my Manolos. During this phase of my career, *en vogue* shoes made me feel grounded, confident, and prepared.

Although the shoe removal here felt far more formal than in the States, the process served as a good icebreaker. Our shoeless feet gathered around a large rectangular board meeting table. I was reading cross-cultural hand gestures, nods, and faint smiles around the room while simultaneously moving through our meeting agenda. At this moment, I knew my communication skills were sharpening. I was all in.

After the meeting, we went back to the hotel to implement edits based on the additional information we obtained. Tired and hungry, I ordered dinner and green tea ice cream for dessert. The ice cream was worth every calorie. As I savored my first ever green tea ice cream experience, I felt energized to be on the other side of the world doing work I truly enjoyed.

The next couple of days flew by as we exchanged revisions. My satisfying moment occurred when I was given the name "Jenny-san" by the clients, who explained to me that in their culture, it is a title of respect. I thanked them. More smiles were reciprocated. It didn't matter that we were from two different countries with two different cultures. Smiles and respect are a universal language when true connection transpires.

It was time to make our way home. As I packed my suitcase, I also stowed away my new experiences in my mind. I had quickly learned some proper Japanese etiquette; cultivated new, respectful client relationships; acquired a new name (Jenny-san); and discovered my love for green tea ice cream.

Back at the New York office, we had about six weeks before our return trip in December to pull this sizable project together into a formal, bound presentation. Effort was full throttle. Attitude was all in, and energy was high-octane. Collectively, our team and the client wanted the valuations to proceed smoothly. Egos and judgment did not run the show. We were doing more than gathering information, running numbers, and preparing reports. We were united in purpose.

Fast-forward to December. In the blink of an eye, I was on a plane, flying to Tokyo again. However, I didn't need the crash course in culture. Instead, I read a book for enjoyment, watched movies, and slept. This time, I was at total ease, looking forward to the grand finale with the clients. I was also craving some of the hotel's decadent green tea ice cream. As long as the presentation books in my luggage made their way off the airplane, I was in fantastic shape.

Time flowed along with my professional development. We were back at the client's office, exchanging bows. My Manolos lined up with the other shoes. I had earned their respect, and they had earned mine. After I distributed the presentation books, I noticed a few nods around the table, which was a good sign. They listened intently during the presentation, nodding more. They did not interrupt. The feedback was positive. Part of the success of this project was that while we were back in New York, we communicated regularly with our client across the world. Updates were shared and expectations managed, which prevented unwelcome surprises.

After the meeting concluded, we were offered a group dinner with the client at a top-end restaurant. Shoes off again. We gathered around a large, low, rectangular table. Conversation flowed while the client leader ordered our dinner. A few minutes later, the servers arrived with large plates of raw fish—exotic to me, mainstream to them.

Suddenly, I felt nervous. Raw sea creatures are *not* my thing. Since it was abundantly clear that this meal was their way of inviting us to experience their culture while expressing gratitude, I wasn't about to offend. At one point, the most senior client leader inquired about why I wasn't eating much. Politely, I replied with something along the lines of "I watch what I eat." He smiled. Once they passed around the sake, I solved my problem with a little bit of eel, which was tolerable for me, followed by a swig of sake. Rinse and repeat. The dinner was engaging, infused with levity and a slight sake-induced buzz.

As we exchanged final goodbyes, I smiled, hearing one last "Jenny-san."

## Reflect

While packing to leave a second time, additional skills were coming with me to supplement my repertoire. My communication abilities extended beyond speaking and hearing words. Now I could listen with my eyes too. Bows and nods spoke as loudly as words. After a friendly introduction to tasteful sake, a bottle to share with friends was flying home with me too.

As the plane ascended, rocketing through the fluffy clouds, a valuable lesson emerged in my mind as the sun shone through the window.

**Collect skills and confidence.**

During the past three months, I hadn't seen obstacles. I focused on opportunities and solutions. I had traveled to Tokyo twice, collecting positive, productive ways to connect cross-culturally with others mutually vested in successful outcomes. Far more experience was unpacked from my suitcase in December than I had packed into that suitcase in October. I knew I belonged in my work, which enabled me to show up in Tokyo wanting to be where I was. In the process, my confidence and business savvy were elevated through my own efforts and attitude.

At this point in my career, I was where I belonged. And when you want to be where you are, you are well-positioned to acquire more knowledge, skills, and self-worth. Somehow it all flows.

> **When you want to be where you are, you are well-positioned to acquire more knowledge, skills, and self-worth.**

Why did I choose to share these Tokyo experiences with you? Because these two trips to the same destination catapulted me to a whole new level of business acumen. The start of the first trip was a bit nerve-wracking. By the end of the second trip, calmness and confidence replaced anxiousness and doubt. That version of Jenny-san was the one who flew home. Acquiring skills comes from navigating experiences, especially challenging, unexpected ones. This lesson gave me the confidence to pursue many opportunities over the past two decades within the worlds of both big business and small business.

Are you actively collecting skills and experiences aligned with you and your business? Or is your "suitcase" too full to pack one more thing? Let's explore how to capture more opportunities that take you higher, not weigh you down.

## Learn

The life of a business owner includes endless responsibilities. You run from one task to the next, one meeting to the next, one trip to the next. With fast-paced, overfilled lives, it's not easy to stop and breathe, let alone think with maximum clarity and a positive attitude.

At the same time, as busy as you are, you want more. You want to grow. Learn. Move forward. Take risks. And you know new experiences open doors to the growth you want. A little bit here, a lot there, and you find yourselves doing things that weren't even on your radar six months ago.

Having a boss and being a leader are two very different experiences. As an employee, your supervisor may tell you to go here or there for a meeting, assign you to a new project, alter your role, and more. As a business owner, however, you are the one deciding what, where, when, who, and how. That distinction alone presents a whole world of fresh opportunities waiting for you to capture. It also means you are the one to develop a strategy for deciding which opportunities align with you and your business.

When faced with a business opportunity, have you ever told yourself:

*Now isn't the right time.*
*I don't have time.*
*I don't have enough help.*
*This will add more stress.*
*It isn't worth it.*
*I'll do it later.*
*I'll have more time when . . .*
*I can't afford it.*
*I won't succeed.*
*I have other priorities (family, pets, parents, and so on).*

Although some of these thoughts may be true some of the time, often they are not. Too often, we think we can't do something just because we haven't done it before. We justify this belief with a list of somewhat exaggerated reasons why we can't. Or we find a reason to do it "later"—knowing "later" often leads to "never."

Yet, if you say yes to every opportunity, you end up submerged, tired, and cranky.

So how do you know when to say yes to an opportunity and when to say no? Unbounded opportunity for growth reside, ironically, in setting limitations. This provides a clear yes and a clear no. You can't say yes to every potentially worthwhile experience at once because you can't be in multiple locations simultaneously. You also won't perform well if you are a total stress case.

On the other hand, you can't say no to everything, either. Whether you enjoy them or not, you must take responsibility for the essential duties that are part of running your business, as well as stretch yourself with new experiences if you want to grow.

The key is to *listen to yourself*. The concept of listening to yourself is a tool I use daily, which I refer to by its acronym LTY. You will see LTY pop up throughout this book. It's the single most valuable business tool you own, and it's accessible to you at any time.

As you explore the fertile grounds where you feel like you belong, LTY. Do not look to others to make your decisions for you. We all have our own yes and our own no. Recognize them. As you do, you can choose the experiences that align with what you can handle effectively at this time in your life. Consequently, the flow of aligned opportunities will increase and your growth will escalate.

## Apply

Here are some practical ways you can LTY to discern when and how to pounce on the next opportunity:

1. **Continue to connect where you feel connected.** Now that you've found where you belong, keep connecting with like-minded folks around you. More worthwhile opportunities will greet you. This is how you learn to apply your skills and confidence to curate the experiences you want.

2. **Identify valuable opportunities.** Not all opportunities are worthwhile. Business owners get pummeled with chances to speak at events at no charge, teach complimentary classes, pay to play, sponsor events and offer swag bags, contribute to publications, guest blog, offer giveaways, and the list goes on, all under the premise of opportunity, business development, lead generation, or exposure.

   Before you say yes or no to these business "opportunities," consider these questions:

   - Does this experience align with you and your business goals? (Aim for a yes.)
   - What is the outcome you're looking to achieve? (Know what you want.)
   - Will this opportunity move you closer to reaching that outcome? (Aim for a yes.)
   - What resources are required to pursue this opportunity? (You need to know the real cost to you.)

3. **Assess risk.** Some experiences are worthwhile, others not so much. Some things you do because it feels good to help others, not to "get" something. Other times, you can spend months of your life and thousands of dollars to get nothing in return.

   Therefore, calculating your return on investment (ROI) can be a useful decision-making tool. ROI is an assessment metric you can use to decide whether to invest financially in an opportunity. Inputs are the gain from investment (or net profit) and cost of investment. The output is a percentage, where a higher percentage indicates a more worthwhile investment, and lower means less so.

$$\text{ROI} = \left( \frac{\text{Gain from Investment} - \text{Cost of Investment}}{\text{Cost of Investment}} \right) \times 100\%$$

   Keep in mind that any formula yields reliable results only if the inputs are accurate. Because we are assessing relative benefits, we don't need to chase precision. I'm mentioning ROI here because it's the thought process that helps you LTY in a business-minded way.

ROI does not eliminate risk or uncertainty. It helps you LTY about how much risk you can afford to accept. When applying the ROI thought process, ask yourself how you could utilize the resources for another opportunity.

The major downside of this ROI calculation method is it doesn't capture time—the precious asset so key for business owners (unless you approximate the value of time as part of the cost of investment). There are other ways to think about ROI, but you're not looking for a finance class. Let's keep moving.

Here we focus on the thought process, not the math, for a simplified example:

**Example:** You are asked to sponsor an event that will cost you $2,500. This is more of a "pay now, build relationships later" type of opportunity if you put in follow-up effort (so for simplicity, the cost of time in this example is 0). However, there is a low probability you will generate tangible profit from it in the foreseeable future.

You need to decide if this opportunity is worth it financially, knowing that your gain from the investment is zero for at least the near term (and may become more "costly" if follow-up effort is required). Here's what this investment looks like on paper if you were to pay for it today:

$$ROI = \left( \frac{\text{Gain from Investment} - \text{Cost of Investment}}{\text{Cost of Investment}} \right) \times 100\%$$

$$ROI = \left( \frac{\$0 - \$2{,}500}{\$2{,}500} \right) \times 100\%$$

$$ROI = -100\%$$

If you also need to spend $3,000 to fly to attend the event and stay at a hotel, the real picture includes the additional cost and turns the $2,500 investment into a $5,500 investment (plus the "cost" of your lost time traveling), yielding more negative financial results.

Accept the reality that if you do this, you will incur a financial loss on this particular investment. This simple math could redirect you toward "no, thanks."

Say you do it anyway. If three months later you generate $15,000 from a client who found you through the event, then the return becomes more fruitful. However, in situations like this, you don't know that upfront.

All decisions are not formula-based. You may choose to base your decisions on your internal risk/reward tolerance. You can compare other investments similarly to reveal what works best for your business. Just remember that not taking a risk is its own risk. Saying no too many times can cost you in terms of quicker growth, a bigger network, or personal and professional development. As you assess risk, avoid both extremes of always saying yes or always saying no with the most valuable tool of all: LTY. Listen to yourself.

4. **Know you are more skilled and capable than you may realize.** When you say yes to the right opportunities, you will rise to the occasion. You will pass the test. You don't need to get an A. You do need to get out there and experience new possibilities to grow yourself and your business.

This process of connecting, spotting, assessing, and knowing doesn't take *all* the angst out of deciding what chances to take and when to take them. Challenges will pop up even when you pursue opportunities that align with you and your business. How do you perform at an optimal level when encountering inevitable snags and self-doubt?

*Listen to yourself (LTY).* When you feel frustrated, overwhelmed, or unsure, return to your most valuable tool: LTY. If you feel like you are doing too much, take a time out. If you're avoiding opportunities with excuses about why you can't, connect with yourself to reveal why. You can be honest with yourself; you are the only one listening. You can stop rationalizing, questioning, and start connecting with yourself.

*Optimize commitment, effort, and attitude as a dynamic trifecta.* Combining the skills of commitment, effort, and attitude can propel you and your business forward like nothing else; it can make or break your outcomes. When you start to feel disconnected, step away for a bit. LTY. Give yourself a break. Then commit to bringing your best effort and attitude to what you're doing.

*Act strategically.* Since you can choose which opportunities you can handle effectively at a given time in your life, you control your strategic speed. At some points, leading your business will require less customer work and more personal focus. Sometimes you will choose to take on fewer new opportunities because you are executing bigger ones with laser focus. You can welcome opportunities as they work for you. Then, when you are connected with yourself enough to hear your internal voice loud and clear, you are well-positioned to connect with others to cultivate relationships. As a result, you open yourself to receive the guidance you need through LTY.

When you're aligned with what you're doing, you will belong when traveling to any destination. Let's pack your bags.

## Act: Unpack, Repack, Repeat

In this exercise, you will unpack and repack your figurative suitcase containing all your professional experiences so you can keep the skills and confidence you've built and let go of all that weighs you down.

1. **Unpack:** Imagine you're unloading the luggage from all your travels—in the form of professional experiences up to this point in your life. What have you been carrying? Make a list of your useful skills, the unique abilities that set you apart, and the unnecessary stuff that weighs you down.

    Your useful and unique skills are a big part of the reason you are a capable business owner. Useful skills are your core abilities that help you lead your business. Unique skills are your differentiating factors.

These attract your ideal customers and colleagues to you, setting you apart from competitors.

Unnecessary baggage is the heavy stuff you carry around in your mind that stifles your development. Here is your chance to unload.

Let's unpack. Examples are included below to get you started.

| Useful | Unique | Unnecessary |
|---|---|---|
| Time management | Listening with eyes | What-ifs |
| Collaborative attitude | Mental stamina | Self-judgment |
|  |  |  |

2. **Pack:** Now pack your bag with the useful and unique skills you want to take with you on your next collection journey. This time, you are replacing unnecessary baggage with focused desires. You are deciding what you seek as you embrace more opportunities to grow you and your business.

The purpose of this part of the exercise is to illustrate that you have much of what you need to acquire more abilities. (I packed LTY for you on this next trip.)

You are lightening your load by focusing on what you need to embrace, do, and collect.

| Useful | Unique | Focused Desires |
|---|---|---|
| Time management | Listening with eyes | Write a book |
| Collaborative attitude | Mental stamina | Launch a new service |
| LTY | Writing | Collaborate with another entrepreneur |
|  |  |  |

## CONQUER OPPORTUNITIES

3. **Repeat:** Going forward, you can repeat this process after each new opportunity. As you acquire more and more knowledge, your useful and unique lists will grow. Meanwhile, your focused desires might change as you elevate yourself to conquer more opportunities.

| Useful | Unique | Focused Desires |
|--------|--------|-----------------|
|        |        |                 |
|        |        |                 |
|        |        |                 |
|        |        |                 |

*Remember, embracing opportunities where you belong can change your whole trajectory. LTY.*

## Ask

1. Think of one unexpected life experience that enabled you to collect useful skills and valuable confidence. How does that noteworthy experience benefit you today?
2. What is one heavy thing you want to unload right now from your figurative suitcase? Is there anything holding you back from offloading it?
3. How will you take action to listen to yourself (LTY) more?

## SOLIDIFY WHAT YOU'VE LEARNED

◊ **LESSON 1:** Change course when a new path feels right.
◊ **LESSON 2:** Collect skills and confidence.

# PART TWO
# CLARIFY: UNDERSTAND YOUR ROLE IN YOUR JOURNEY

Do you feel more connected with yourself?

In Part One, you learned that your ability to connect with yourself and others is one of your greatest assets. When you discover where you belong and accumulate skills and confidence, you notice the sun peeking through the clouds as understanding becomes clearer and brighter.

Throughout this journey, the most critical concept to keep top of mind is LTY. As you continue to practice LTY, this asset will become a high-value strength. Naturally, the more you LTY to align your business with the real you, additional questions will pop into your head. How can you become even more effective as a business leader? What role are you meant to play, and how can you maximize your strengths?

The next two chapters explore the theme of clarity, each highlighting a lesson related to understanding your role in your journey. When you know where you belong, you are prepared to identify your strengths and show up the way you want. With full ownership of your strengths, you can then focus to win.

Let's clarify your role in your business and your life.

## CHAPTER 3
# OPTIMIZE YOUR PERFORMANCE

Have you ever gained clarity by changing your work environment, even for a few hours or days?

Previously, I found where I belonged working at global corporate consulting firms and in corporate finance roles. At this point in my career, my work environment was beginning to feel like a cage. Command-and-control leadership styles dominated.

I didn't realize how trapped I truly felt until I boarded a plane in Newark, New Jersey, for a field visit. My first clue was my happiness level. I can't recall ever feeling energized to be on a plane for a work trip; however, I welcomed the cramped airplane as opposed to my spacious work office. Here, I was in close quarters, breathing recycled air, sitting next to a complete stranger, yet I felt totally free, as if I was inhaling fresh oxygen.

A few hours later, I landed at a major airport. After walking for what felt like miles, I retrieved my rental car. My global travel instincts kicked into gear as I navigated the steps involved seamlessly. This was my first time traveling in this corporate role. It felt pleasant to be out of the confines of the office, employing some of my underutilized skills.

Although I had been to this city for work years prior, I had never driven through it. I turned on the radio and got into a zone. Suddenly, I heard something hit the windshield. I jumped in my seat, clenching the steering wheel. Then I noticed large balls of hail, somewhere between the size of grapes and golf balls, falling from the bright blue sky. Sheets of hail. I'd never seen anything like it. A hailstorm in June? Yes, it was common in this part of the States. As the hail pelted the car, I smiled, thinking, "Jen, it's all part of the experience." The hail didn't stop me from finding my way.

The purpose of this trip was to tour a few area facilities, meet operations specialists, and exchange information. For me, it wasn't about checking boxes or telling the field how to do things differently. I wasn't there to uncover more profit or review capital expenditure requests. This visit was about going beyond titles and roles. Human connection was my primary goal. For the next few days, I intended to drive results through connection, meaning, and kindness. I wanted to do my work, my way.

Before calling it a night, I spent some time getting organized for the next day. Always one to plan, I made sure to pack tops, pants, and jackets that were professional and comfortable. My soft-soled flats traveled with me this time instead of heels, since I'd be on the move. My style had to convey approachability and practicality. I would be meeting operations associates I had only talked to on the phone or didn't know at all. My first face-to-face impression would help set the tone for what followed.

Around seven the next morning, I left the hotel in my rental car to drive about an hour and twenty minutes to see field associates. I felt a spring in my step that I hadn't felt since my global consulting days. I turned on the radio and once again got into my zone. I pondered what approachability might look like to operations team members meeting a home office executive. I didn't know how the situation would unfold until I was living it. So I decided not to spend time anticipating scenarios. I enjoyed the gorgeous, picturesque scenery and a good local rock radio station.

When I got closer to my destination, I stopped to fuel myself with coffee. I needed another large cup to perk up for the long day ahead.

As I drove, I observed the bright blue sky and puffy clouds. The sun peeked through. No hailstorm surprises this time. Here I was, driving by myself on an open road about 1,800 miles from my home office, feeling fabulous. It was the perfect road for a sports car. I enjoyed it nonetheless—in my bland rental sedan.

Safe arrival. I finished my last sip of coffee and eagerly grabbed my belongings out of the car. I passed through check-in and security. It felt good to step out of my world, into theirs. Going to work felt exciting rather than mundane. My sensations of stagnation evaporated. My inner voice told me this was going to be a memorable day.

Warm greetings surrounded me. Eye contact revealed genuineness. Colleagues toured me around while telling me about their work. The humble pride in their voices was discernible. I wanted to learn about what they did directly from them, not from some report or from their boss or from their boss's boss. I was being me. I cared. There was no corporate veil or pretense. In turn, it was apparent that they appreciated this visit from New Jersey.

The next morning, I woke up before sunrise, enthusiastic about starting another day of visits. As part of the intentional design of the day, I would be leading the monthly financial operations discussions from one of the sites instead of from the corporate office. I conducted the discussions with the operations directors while gathered around a table, which made the meetings more pleasant. I was able to listen, observe, and participate while in the same room with the ones responsible for reporting the numbers.

We shared meals, during which real conversations unfolded. This was beyond refreshing for me. At this point in my role back home, I was churning out an enormous amount of work while eating lunch at my large, dark wood desk every day.

We shared valuable information. There were no emails, spreadsheets, formal presentations, or anyone micromanaging me. There was engagement, dialogue, candor, and a few good laughs.

As my last night came to a close, it was time to pack my suitcase. A happy-sad emotion washed over me. I had conquered the opportunity presented to me. I was fulfilled by the positive vibes of the past few days. However, I felt downcast, knowing in all likelihood, I wouldn't be back out there to see the same folks, with whom I had truly enjoyed spending time. I was tucking away more than my clothes and toiletries.

A deeper connection to myself and additional experiences were coming home with the stronger, refreshed version of me.

## Reflect

While driving the rental car back to the airport the next morning, I processed what had transpired over the last few days. As the warm sun beamed through the car windows, I soaked in my surroundings one last time. I knew that quite a bit inside me had shifted for the best.

I continued to think while going through the typical airport travel motions. Boarding the plane home, I felt different. More connected. Lighter.

As the plane took off, I took a deep breath. The air didn't feel stale. Perhaps it was because I felt refreshed. My newfound clarity was accompanying me home, wrapping me like a warm, fuzzy blanket.

Reflecting on the last few days, I thought about my encounters in terms of connections, conversations, laughs, and smiles, rather than numbers, reports, or tasks. I had gained a new outlook about myself, my abilities, and my worth, made possible because I was connected with myself—and then connected well with others.

I knew I had amassed useful skills and knowledge through my years of work and personal experience. However, this experience led me to get more intimate with my strategic strengths. Now I realized that my kindness had emerged as a natural leadership strength. Those I met during the last few days interacted with me positively because of the human way I showed up. I arrived as myself rather than as a corporate executive version of myself. And I discovered a key lesson.

**Let the strength of kindness flow through you.**

One of the primary reasons my business trip was so productive and enjoyable was that genuine kindness prevailed. It was a vibe. It was palpable. It was real. On site, each of us was performing within our zone of strength. The operations specialists were in their element, educating me by showing me what they do. I was there to listen, learn, and share knowledge. Operating within our strengths made it easy for all of us to display mutual respect. We were kind. And this kindness, in turn, made it easy for all of us to continue working from our strengths.

Contrary to what some want you to believe, kindness is not weakness. This experience taught me that kindness is an advantageous business strength that enables others to live in their strength zone *and* is a branch of operating within our strengths. Some have it; some don't. Those who do have it strengthen everyone around them.

Why did I share this experience with you? Because this trip was a turning point in my business leadership journey and my career. At the start of the trip, I connected with myself and made the commitment to do work my way. I decided I would show up as myself, not some executive version of me.

By the time I touched down back in New Jersey, I was a different version of myself. I had gained clarity on my strategic strengths. And the catalyst was simply changing my work environment for a few days.

As a result, I now understood more about my role in my journey. My strengths were mine to use, which was what I planned to do going forward. I knew I was on a new path now; it reminded me of how I had transformed my trajectory to business from science.

This lesson enabled me to tap confidently into my kindness as a strength. It also inspired me to inventory my unique abilities to be used for the betterment of myself and others. I could maximize what I had and improve what I chose to develop.

Imagine the ways we could elevate ourselves and each other if we all let kindness flow through us to others.

Are you operating from a place of kindness in ways that enhance your business life for you, your team, and your customers?

## Learn

Understanding your role and your learnings in your journey is so critical *and powerful.*

There isn't a distinction between who you are as a business owner and who you are in all the other roles you play. As business professionals running around all day, it is challenging to view yourself in a big picture way when you are faced with a constantly growing list of to-dos.

Have you felt like your work environment is growing stagnant and mundane? Have you felt like you're drained by unhelpful personalities in your environment?

If so, that can turn into feeling like:

- I'm understaffed.
- I'm overutilized.
- I'm undervalued.
- I'm bogged down.
- I'm stressed out.
- I'm tired.

Some days you feel too exhausted to be kind. You're not alone. This is a flashing red light that you are operating in your survival zone rather than your strength zone. Perform for another day. Quelch the work fires. Keep multiple balls in the air.

Meanwhile, you're not a trained circus act. You need peace to refresh your mind to refocus. Your brain and body are calling for a break. Give it to them. When suboptimal feelings and thoughts sneak in, it signals a need to step away to simplify. It's time to alter your scenery. A few minutes, a few hours, a few days—take whatever you can when you can grab it. Keep in mind a change of surroundings does not have to cost any money. It can also be spent as you desire.

LTY to identify your strengths, turn up your performance level, and unlock your zone of kindness. As you listen to yourself, you may uncover thoughts, feelings, and beliefs that others or situations are using to hold you back, intentionally or not. Having a boss and being a leader present different hurdles. As an employee, your supervisor may try to tell you, or others on your behalf, your strengths and weaknesses. They may box you in accordingly. Some may even see you excel at certain things and assume that is what you need to keep doing. This could prevent you from shining.

As a business owner, *you* are your leader. You possess the inner capability to lead with your strengths and with kindness. You don't need additional research and facts to convince you to be kind. You already know its value.

> **Leading with kindness makes you and your business stronger.**

Each small business is unique. Business owners run their shows according to their distinct values, principles, personality, and priorities. To identify and tap into your strengths strategically, you don't have to analyze and alter your habits and behaviors. You're not setting out to change who you are. Following the theme of Part Two, your objective here is to *clarify* your role in your independent journey.

How do you know what strengths to tap into more? You conduct an honest assessment of yourself. You review your strengths and any opportunities for development. As a small business owner, you likely do not have a formal corporate human resources department regularly rolling out performance appraisals and leadership review processes. For this task, you don't need those. You can play this role for yourself and your company.

As you take stock of you, LTY. Do not look to others to tell you what you do well—or not so well. They aren't in your mind. They aren't running your business. They aren't living your life. Deep down, you already know your capabilities. Don't doubt them and don't limit them. Fully utilize them.

Also, remember that kindness is an advantageous strength itself that shines when you are operating within your strengths. *Kindness is strong*.

Leading with kindness makes you and your business stronger. As you lead this way, you will elevate your strengths, yourself, and your business.

## Apply

Here are some practical ways you can LTY about kindness and identify both your key strengths and any opportunities to tap into additional ones:

1. **Identify your key strengths.** Entrepreneurs typically share three unique overarching abilities:

    Courage—to carve disruptive paths.
    Creativity—to craft unique offerings.
    Curiosity—to explore value opportunities.

    These are the powers that propelled you to where you are. Now you are digging deeper to pinpoint the strengths that enable you to run your business effectively, with ease.
    For the purposes of this chapter, the fastest, easiest way to spot your strengths is to ask yourself two straightforward kindness (toward yourself) questions:
    *What do I love to do for my business that doesn't feel like work?*
    Some enjoy doing their own social media marketing. They are founders and business owners of service businesses, not marketing agencies. However, they excel at certain advertising tactics that drive revenue generation because their strong passion shines through. If it benefits your business and your contentment level, keep going.
    *What do I wake up eager to do for work?*
    For entrepreneurial authors or editors, writing comes to mind. An owner of a music or fitness studio may be passionate about teaching classes or developing new ones.

2. **Know your highest value strengths**. Not all strengths hold equal weight for your business. The treasured ones are connected to kindness and help shape your unique value proposition as a business owner and for your business overall.

   To determine your highest-value business strengths, consider these questions for each:

   - Does this strength align with you and your business goals?
     (Aim for yes.)
   - Does this strength serve your business well today, tomorrow, and beyond?
     (Aim for yes.)
   - Is this strength required to run your business?
     (Aim for yes. Otherwise, it's a hobby, like chef-quality meal preparations or professional-caliber dog grooming if you run a consulting business. You get the point.)
   - Does your strength contribute to your revenue, your profit (perhaps by reducing expenses), or both?
     (It's useful to understand how your strength translates into monetary value.)

3. **Let kindness flow through your business as a strategic strength.** There is room for kindness in every business. Business results can be kinder, more purposeful, and more profitable simultaneously. Although there is no one-size-fits-all approach, nearly every business has untapped potential to offer more kindness to its customers, team, vendors, and even its owner (you). Are you serving your clients by combining your highest value strengths with kindness in words and actions?

   Operating from your other strategic strengths can naturally unlock the flow of kindness. You can be a strong, kind leader, guiding others through challenges in a very human, connected way. Create kindness your way. Let's look at some simple elements of kindness that can thrive in small businesses:

*Embody goodness.* Do you demonstrate acts of kind leadership? Do you show that you can step into your power while leading with compassion, understanding, and patience?

*Add levity to situations.* You can deliver intended messages in an enjoyable, lighthearted manner. Have you ever attended a conference with speakers who droned on about how important and wonderful they were? Be the opposite of that. Bring uplifting laughter. Bring warm smiles. Bring gentle eye contact.

*Welcome warmly.* Your customers and your team deserve to feel welcome, respected, and valued. Negative impressions are detrimental to any business. Anyone in direct communication with customers best be friendly and well-mannered.

*Express gratitude.* Say thank you—and mean it. Show appreciation to your customers with a small gift, write a thank-you note, engage on social media, or more. So many miss the importance of this (and what it reveals about them).

*Show you care.* Do you and your team convey a sense of caring for your customers? For example, is the sales team pushing folks to sign up for services or buy products that aren't the best options for their needs? More customers can see through this than you may think.

*Communicate with your clientele.* Ask your customers for feedback. Ask what would make them happier doing business with you. Simple surveys can be valuable information-gathering tools. Be open to exploring findings, even if you don't like what they say.

4. **Be kind and true to yourself.** Your goal here is to stay true to you—not to modify yourself. Every business owner has weaknesses because everyone does not excel at everything. A weakness of yours could be another business owner's strength, and vice versa. That's okay. The key is to be honest with yourself about where you are and who you are, where you want to go and who you want to be. LTY. You will find that kindness makes it easier to LTY.

    Weaknesses that are embedded in your personality are part of you. This means they are part of your business. For this reason, think of your weaknesses with kindness for yourself and simply be aware of them. For certain types of businesses, a leader's weakness can be a strength in a different context. For example, an introvert won't excel as the face of a company in charge of business development efforts like networking events, video interviews, or lead generation meetings. On the other hand, an introvert could be a gifted inventor, scientist, best-selling author, researcher, and much more.

Some behaviors stemming from years of habits combined with personality are challenging. Be mindful of these to conduct yourself accordingly. For instance, some business owners are not early risers. If you know this about yourself, don't schedule meetings at 8:30 in the morning. At the same time, don't expect the person you are trying to do business with to be available for you at 6:00 in the evening because they may have been awake since 5:00 a.m.

Although you can deemphasize, mitigate, and accept your weaknesses, that is not the focus here. The focus here is to strengthen you and your business while letting kindness flow through you to others.

LTY. Get real with the real you to acknowledge what can help you elevate yourself and your business. You can assemble your personalized strengths toolkit to bring to any situation. Let's select your tools and be sure to include kindness.

## Act: Assemble Your Strengths Toolkit

You are now prepared to start assembling your toolkit in two steps:

1. **Identify your strategic strengths.** As you assemble your strengths toolkit, keep in mind that strategic strengths aren't confined to the work world. For business owners, career and personal lives blend.

    Some useful and unique skills that you identified in Chapter 2's exercise may reappear in your strengths column. This exercise is intended to go deeper. Focus on your strengths that give you

# ALIGN YOUR BUSINESS WITH THE REAL YOU

differentiating competitive advantages as a business owner.

Remember, you don't need to excel at everything in all facets of your business and life. Be honest with yourself. Some strengths you need to elevate your business you can fill in through strategic delegation. We'll talk more about delegation in Chapter 12.

Also, by this point, you may have started to develop your skill of LTY. So you may want to list LTY as one of your strengths or commit to transforming LTY to a strength. Try to not over index on strategic strengths. Bullets and not run on sentences are the goal.

| Identify Strategic Strengths |
|---|
| Crafting unique offerings |
| Exploring value opportunities |
| Solving problems |
| Personalizing solutions |
| Leading with kindness |
| Expressing courtesies |
| Utilizing mental stamina |
| LTY |

2. **Choose how kindness flows in your business.** Kindness enables you to work stronger, more connected with yourself and others. Your capacity for kindness is an excellent diagnostic and a sign of working in alignment with your strengths. Where does kindness flow in your business? Are you tapping into kindness as a strength? How are you demonstrating kindness?

Let's begin. Examples are included below to help get you started.

| **Make Kindness a Strategic Strength** |
| --- |
| Saying consistently please and thank you (and meaning it) |
| Expressing gratitude toward clients |
| Showing appreciation for your team—and caring for them |
| Adding levity to the workday |
| Expressing interest in your clients' and team members' work |
| Respecting others' time (don't schedule meetings at 3 p.m. on a Friday in the summer) |
| Being generous within your means—it's not all about you |
| Giving to others in alignment with the real you |

*Remember, you can choose to allow kindness to flow through you and your business as a strategic strength.*

## Ask

1. How has the concept "kindness is strong" shown up in your life? In your business?
2. Where do you like to go to reset your mind for a few minutes, hours, or days?

## SOLIDIFY WHAT YOU'VE LEARNED

◊ **LESSON 1:** Change course when a new path feels right.

◊ **LESSON 2:** Collect skills and confidence.

◊ **LESSON 3:** Let the strength of kindness flow through you.

## CHAPTER 4
# FOCUS TO WIN

Have you ever experienced a sudden, unexpected, life-altering event that will remain ingrained in your mind forever?

On March 12, 2008, I was walking from my office to the train station like any normal weeknight evening. Feeling a bit uncomfortable, I stopped to set my computer bag down. After taking a long, intentional breath and stretching a bit, I picked up my bag and continued trekking along.

I boarded the train, looking forward to resting my tired eyes for forty-five minutes. The good thing about riding a crowded public train to and from work was that it gave me a forced timeout. It was a mandatory break from the grind.

Early the next morning, I woke up feeling good. I worked out like normal. That night, my husband and I enjoyed a nice date-night dinner at a delicious little Italian restaurant. Life felt happy.

Less than twelve hours later, my body jarred me awake around four in the morning with pains. Pains that I had never felt before. Pains that didn't feel right. Pains like I didn't want to move an inch.

I woke up my husband. He tried to assure me I was okay. I breathed and prayed, but nothing was helping. My body kept screaming. About half an hour later, I finally listened to what my body was saying. I said to

Mark, "I'm calling the doctor." I talked to my doctor, who transmitted his calm, comforting demeanor through the phone line. He instructed me to go to the ER. He said he'd meet us there.

We threw on our clothes and went out the door. The drive to Saint Barnabas Medical Center (now Cooperman Barnabas Medical Center) felt like it took forever. The car moved forward, but time felt frozen. With every pain, I clenched the passenger door handle. I tried to maintain composure. I had to relax or else I wasn't sure what would happen.

As I glanced to my left, I noticed Mark was observing my squirms and door-handle clenches, then glancing at the clock. I thought to myself, *This is real; he knows it's real.* Mark had been a volunteer firefighter for many years. He knew how to stay calm and resolve problems under intense pressure. However, seeing him admit with complete silence that there was a real issue now told me we had an unavoidable situation to navigate together.

While we waited in the ER exam room, we held hands, united in love. We were also holding onto hope and faith that everything would work out well. We made a formidable team, so we knew we were capable of dealing with the unknown now unfolding.

I breathed a sigh of relief when my doctor walked through the doorway. As our eyes met, he smiled. His presence in the room helped me relax. I returned a smile through the frightening pain. After assessing the situation, the expert in the room said to my husband and me, "You're having your baby within the next twenty-four hours." That sentence is forever etched in my mind.

Gasping for air, I replied, "What? I'm not due until May 5th!" I blurted out, "I worked today, and I worked out this morning. I was fine."

"You're not fine now," my doctor replied.

As another pain zapped my body like a lightning bolt, I knew he was right.

That was then; this was *now*. This major life event forced me to live in the now. I panicked about what this all meant. My husband and I locked eyes. Would our baby be okay?

My mind continued to spiral. My thoughts scattered, replaced by the many worries and fears piling up in my head. I even wandered into trivial territory: *Our baby's room isn't done. The furniture hasn't arrived. We don't have clothing for a preemie.* Realizing these concerns were meaningless, I cast them all aside.

After addressing our important, heavy questions and doubts, my doctor assigned me one job. "Stay calm." He instructed me to forget work. Forget email. Forget all of that (he knew me well).

The if/then statement became crystal clear in my mind: If I focus on winning for our baby, then this will go well. If I don't focus now, then the outcome may be bad. The highest stakes game of my life had begun.

*Focus, Jen; focus.*

These were not sexy moments. I was confined to a bed wearing an unattractive hospital gown. I was not allowed to get up. I wasn't permitted to consume anything other than water, ice chips, and the IV. I didn't care about food. I got used to the pain. All I cared about was our baby.

The next twenty-four hours were critical. Our baby's lungs had not developed yet, which was nerve-wracking. The medical team administered something so my body would stop going into labor. My doctor, who was quickly becoming a medical hero in my eyes, made it clear he was devoted to our care. He explained our baby's lungs could be boosted by giving me two shots, spaced a certain number of hours apart; one dose was better than none. Getting both was best for the baby's health. Every morsel of energy I had was converted to determination to hold on long enough to get both shots.

During this time, my role was to keep my body relaxed. Shot one done. We were halfway to the finish line. My devoted husband didn't leave my side. He also resolved to claim victory as a healthy family.

Meanwhile, we were told our baby would not be leaving the hospital with us. He needed to stay in the NICU for an estimated four weeks. As much as this news stung, we knew it was the best for our child. We also knew the NICU at Cooperman Barnabas Medical Center had earned an outstanding reputation. Our baby was in good hands.

At that point, we made a couple of phone calls to inform the soon-to-be grandparents what was happening. Of course, they were alarmed. We asked them gently not to come to the hospital. My husband and I were committed to staying calm and focusing on our son as a unified team of three.

I was fixated on achieving the best for this precious, innocent life inside of me. I tuned into my body, talking to it silently and out loud, coaxing it to protect our little one. Funny thing is I had to limit talking to the baby because whenever I talked to him, he would wiggle around and do his "happy feet," which was more activity than we wanted.

However, I was comforted to know, to feel, that despite what was happening, he was happy there. So I serenely visualized our son's laughter, hugs, and smiles. For the next few hours, our tranquil breathing was in sync as peacefulness flowed through my body to his and back again.

Early Saturday morning, March 15, my doctor came to visit us. Since it wasn't quite time to deliver our baby, he was heading to the St. Patrick's Day parade with his family for a couple of hours. He assured us he would be back to deliver our son. I admired his calm confidence, which convinced me he had read my situation and still felt comfortable enough to attend the parade. We exchanged more smiles. Then he scurried off to join his family.

At this point, both of those critical shots were flowing through my veins and into our son's little body, working their medical magic. I channeled calm confidence while being present with my husband and son. An absolute sense of peace washed over me. Mark and I held hands and prayed.

The next part was less peaceful, so let's fast-forward to 4:53 p.m. when our son Richard Mark entered the world at five pounds and seventeen-and-a-half inches. This was considered a blessing for a preemie. Our May 5 due date had been unexpectedly moved up to March 15. We still had our lucky number five in there. My mom's favorite number is five. And Richard was named after my calm, strong, and steady father, Richard.

We held our safe, precious baby for the first time. His head was the size of my husband's palm. His soft, tiny fingers grabbed onto my pinky while he glanced into my eyes and smiled. I will never forget that dear pinky hug or first smile. We knew he'd be strong. We prayed he'd be healthy and happy.

A sudden rush of feelings arrived next. Relief. Elation. Fatigue. Peace. Victory.

## Reflect

We achieved team victory as a family, forever bonded together. As I processed this beautifully intense experience, the lesson landed.

**Stay driven in the moment to excel under pressure.**

This realization extends beyond tapping into strengths. The ability to stay driven *and* stay present under intense pressure is far more difficult than it sounds. (Ask me how I know.) This lesson solidifies the difference between winning what you want or losing because you slid out of your peak performance zone.

Seconds matter. Minutes matter. Thoughts matter. Breaths matter. It all matters in the present because being focused to win fuels you to stay driven to excel no matter what pressure you face.

What inspired me to share such a personal, non-work-related experience in a business book? At first, I hesitated. Then I decided to go all in and share the unexpected ways I had learned about finding my peak performance zone so you can find yours.

> **Our most powerful life lessons don't just apply to some of our roles. They change who we are and how we show up in every role.**

Our most powerful life lessons don't just apply to some of our roles. They change who we are and how we show up in *every* role. We might learn an important life lesson when we are in caregiver mode, and we can then take that lesson with us to work to strengthen our performance.

As a result of my game-changing experience in that hospital bed, I realized that staying driven in the moment to perform well under pressure meant I had to tune out what wasn't important and tune into me. This lesson accompanied me to work through my increased ability to stay engaged in what I'm doing when I'm doing it to deliver excellence consistently.

This lesson requires discipline. It takes heart. If I hadn't fully tuned into myself and what I had to accomplish in all those seconds and all those minutes during those twenty-four hours of labor, I would have sacrificed the health of my precious baby. Nothing, nothing distracted me from staying focused on the task at hand. You can do the same.

You don't have to be a parent to absorb this lesson. We all experience high-pressure events, some of which are life-changing. When we stay driven to turn up the effort in tough situations, we allow ourselves to achieve astonishing feats. If you don't focus on what you want, you waste your time and mental and physical resources, reducing your successes.

Do you like to win? I do. When something you care about is at stake, winning is worthwhile. Winning advances you to the next level. And let's face it, winning is fun. Let's learn how to align your business and yourself to focus on winning by tuning into what matters most.

## Learn

Business owners must focus to win. If you don't stay driven to perform under pressure, you miss opportunities to win the short game and the long game in business and life. You're already familiar with the pressures of being an entrepreneur, some of which may make you wonder why you signed up for this in the first place:

- Know your customer.
- Serve your clients.
- Build your brand.
- Assemble your team.
- Formulate your strategy.

- Develop new business.
- Deliver the presentation.
- Close the deal.
- Invest in your business.
- Retain talent.
- Bring in revenue.
- Address pricing constraints.
- Revamp the product/service mix.
- Stay up-to-date with technology.
- Grow profits.
- Reinvest in your business.
- Scale your business.
- Ignore the critics.
- Support loved ones.

On top of the pile of business pressures, you have a personal life with its own demands. For example, running a business while caring for your family adds stress on top of stress. Plus, you are aware of the importance of taking care of yourself by eating healthy, exercising, and getting a good night's sleep. Knowing you need a good night's sleep as your wide-awake eyes stare at the ceiling can add even more pressure.

Now thinking about your stress level is making you more stressed. Can you relate?

As you set out to perform amid mounting pressures, you inevitably get interrupted or distracted. Then noise drowns out your quiet, controlled thoughts. In daily business life, what does this noise look like and feel like?

Well, it goes something like this: You're working on the one thing you want to get done. Then you are interrupted. You start doing something else or talking to someone else or looking at your phone or thinking about something else that doesn't need to be top of mind for you. Your flow is broken.

Situations can be "noisy" if you are at a crucial moment and must prioritize one thing at all costs to reach your finish line. Interruptions and the resulting distractions, or noise, can be external or internal. Some are intended; some are not. All noise isn't necessarily bad or negative.

For example, let's say you are concentrating, working toward a deadline. You are interrupted by your phone ringing. Unexpectedly, your loved one needs a ride somewhere or is sick or injured. You need to swoop into caregiver mode. In that moment, your center of attention shifts to winning in caregiver mode so you can return to winning in business owner mode later. Or you are working at your office, storefront, or home, locked in focus, and someone pops by, unexpectedly breaking your flow. It's possible they don't get that you were in the middle of real work. Although both interruptions were not intentional on your part, they were still interruptions.

More commonly, as you keep moving toward your goals, internal distractions pop up. Typically, business owners have multiple work streams to manage simultaneously. You may be doing one thing at work, but then your mind drifts to another approaching deadline, an upcoming business meeting, or an employee issue.

To make things more complicated, the internal self-inflicted thought interruptions cross over from work to personal, and vice versa. You're trying to prioritize work, but your mind is distracted by thoughts about other stuff transpiring in your life, like your upcoming family move, the disrupting renovations in your home, the sad passing of a loved one, packing your son or daughter for college, caring for elderly parents, cooking dinner that night, or a thousand other things.

Whether intentional or unintentional, internal or external, these examples all have one thing in common. They are distracting in ways that affect your flow. They can have a detrimental effect on your work performance. The key is learning how to stay driven in the moment to achieve what you want.

Critical life situations, on the other hand, have a way of forcing us to focus. Life is wonderful—until it's not. In the blink of an eye, you are greeted with an unwelcome dire situation. You go into preterm labor. Someone close to you needs emergency surgery or is diagnosed with cancer. You lose an inner circle member. In some ways, it can be easier for you to focus because you can think of nothing else.

When situations aren't life-threatening, how do you focus on winning despite interruptions? LTY. Remember, LTY is the single most valuable business tool you own. It's accessible to you at any time and in any place. You own it within you.

LTY will help you stay driven in the moment to excel under pressure. You learn to tune out the distractions. Then you gain laser-like focus.

## Apply

Despite the daily pressures of business ownership, you can apply the tool of LTY to spot and reduce distractions, which will help you decrease the noise in your life. Since distractions that create noise can be external or internal, and intended or unintended, it's helpful to identify common sources of distractions as well as some examples:

1. **External distractions** can include your phone buzzing, email or text alerts, employee issues, client demands, unexpected visitors, impromptu meetings, family needs, social media, and more. External distractions will always be there. The key is to spot them and tune them out when you need or want to focus on something else.
2. **Internal distractions** are self-inflicted. Anytime you are doing one thing and thinking about another, you are distracting yourself. It's even more intense when your mind is racing about something going on in your business or life.

    Internal distractions zap your needed energy. You spend mental resources interrupting your own thoughts with worries, ruminations, what-if scenarios, and more. You may even expend so much mental energy that your physical body suffers and you feel tired, achy, sick, or some other avoidable sensation. How can you stay driven to excel under pressure if you have no energy? In this case, the problem is not someone or something else. It's you. You are unintentionally preventing your own wins.

3. **Intended distractions** can be external or internal. For example, certain types create distractions for others purposefully because they use noise as a strategy. They want to get in your head. One example is in the context of sports. A teammate talks nonsense to you before you go onto the field or up to bat. The opposing team jeers your team during the game.

    Now, take this concept from the field to the game of business. In the business world, the intentional noise creator can be the boss who tries to throw you off-kilter before a meeting with higher-ups (so you enter the room off-balance). It can be the supervisor who excludes you from the meeting where all the work you did will be reviewed and discussed (so it's easier for them to take credit). It can be the colleague who doesn't include you on the meeting agenda circulated before a meeting in which you must perform (so you aren't as prepared or well-spoken). It can be the boss who is in the background, working against you when you're up for a promotion (to protect their insecurities).

    As a small business owner, the intentional distractor can be an overly demanding client, problematic employee, or jealous competitor. Once you spot the intended distractions, you become more aware of them every step of the way. In turn, you apply LTY to stop the noise before it starts.

4. **Unintended distractions** happen in the normal course of daily life, creating noise that no one intends. For instance, you are trying to work from home and your kid or parent needs you. (Maybe they don't really need you. At that moment, they think they do.) You get distracted. Your concentration is broken. Now you hear noise in your mind about how you have more to do, you didn't get done what you needed to do, or whatever else you tell yourself. The point is these distractions happen without poor intentions.

    In addition, there are many times when you distract yourself unintentionally with your thoughts. You may be working on a project. Then you distract yourself with a carryover thought from an earlier situation. Next, you hold on to that distracting thought to second-guess yourself about a business decision you made that day. As you're working, you may find yourself listening to thoughts like:

*I should have said this.*
*I should have done it differently.*
*I should have prepared more.*
*I should have said no.*
*I should have said yes.*

You get the idea. Nothing helpful comes from thinking, "I should have."

You don't intend to distract yourself. You don't mean to second-guess yourself. You don't plan to ruminate. You don't want to break your concentration and get in your way. However, you do unintentionally from time to time. So how do you reduce the noise to focus on what you need to do?

You can zero in on how to manage external and internal distractions (whether intended or unintended) before the noise gets loud. Even when work and personal external and internal distractions cross over from one to the other, you can still stay driven in the moment to excel under pressure.

**External distractions** can be mitigated when you identify them ahead of time and plan accordingly. In essence, you are putting other things aside to focus on what you must get done when it must get done. Let's walk through three examples:

- You run your business in person at your office, store, or studio. Your concentration is broken day after day by customers who walk in and demand your time and employees who interrupt you when you are in the middle of something else. Typically, the culprits lack self-awareness, are impatient, think they are doing their job, or view their stuff as more important than your stuff. How do you keep your sanity?

*Spot the patterns.* Usually there are one or two employees or clients that press the most demands on your time. Identify them.

*Communicate what you want.* Communication is everything. The point is to spot the pattern, identify the sources of interruption, and communicate to mitigate.

For instance, do you want your assistant to stop interrupting you when you are with a client? Do you want your demanding client to schedule time with you rather than suck your time with their impromptu calls or visits? You can politely excuse yourself from the demands by saying you have another matter to attend to. Then remove yourself from their grip.

- You are working from home. You have client work to complete and submit that night to meet a deadline to which you agreed. What do you do?

  *Plan ahead.* Whatever you can do in advance to help yourself, do it. Prepare meals ahead of time. Don't schedule appointments for yourself during your focus time. Give your dogs a long walk so they sleep while you work. Help yourself before your crunch period.

  *Communicate in advance.* Tell your friends or family that you are going off the radar to focus on a project. They can survive without you for a time. If they can't, then arrange additional help in advance.

- You are interrupted by folks in your business or personal life who want to make sure they win instead of you. These types turn up the noise as a tactic to distract you or make you feel less valuable or worthy. How do you deal?

  *Limit involvement.* Identify the culprits. You know who they are. Then dial down the noise by limiting your involvement with them. It doesn't mean you can't talk to them or be around them. Recognize it's best for you to stay tuned into what makes you feel good, magnifies your strengths, and allows kindness to flow.

  *Ignore, ignore. Ignore.* Once you observe what is happening, you can ignore it to preserve your energy. Let their backhanded compliments, rude comments, or bragging roll right off. See it for what it is: nonsense. Once you recognize the noisy behavior as their problem and not yours, you win the game every time. Go for the win.

**Internal distractions** can be prevented when you quiet your mind. How the heck do you quiet your unintentionally noisy mind? *Listen to yourself.* LTY to acknowledge what you're saying to yourself. Perhaps there is some intuitive guidance you need to hear. Sort through it. Observe it. Then let it go.

Next, tell yourself, *I'm all in to focus on this*. As other thoughts pop into your mind, and they will, you instruct them to leave. Create a mantra for yourself like, "Now focus," or "Stay driven," or "Focus to win."

When you apply your ability to focus to win, you waste no opportunities. Let's visualize your wins.

## Act: Visualize the Win

At this point, you are ready to spot and reduce distractions to reduce noise in your life. You want to win consistently. With more focused effort, you will.

1. **Assess your distractions.** Recognize that you don't have control over all the distractions that may arise, so you can't prevent all of them from occurring. However, you can identify your biggest problem areas to help yourself.

    In the boxes below, rank your performance distractions from one to four, with one being the top distraction and four being the lowest.

    For example, unintentional internal distractions may be your biggest barriers if your mind tends to fire on all cylinders at all times. Intentional internal distractions may be third if you've learned to limit your intentional distractions. Unintentional external distractions may be second, if that's how you feel your life's been lately.

If you have mastered the skill of not caring what others do or say to you or about you, intentional external distractions may be your lowest with a number four in that box. (On the contrary, if that stuff gets you off-kilter, you might rank it as one.)

**Performance Distractions**

| Rank 1–4<br>1 Top Distraction,<br>4 Lowest | Intentional | Unintentional |
|---|---|---|
| External | | |
| Internal | | |

2. **Customize your training.** Your top two ranked categories are where you need to train. You need to develop your customized practice routine for focus so you can apply it when it counts.

    For example, if external categories are more distracting for you, train here to get stronger. If internal categories rank higher because you tend to interrupt yourself more often than others distract you, then that's where you need to devote effort.

    This is where visualization will serve as your personal trainer. Let's get started.

3. **Visualize your win.** Visualization can help you prepare to excel.

    First, you are going to recall a bad business experience. Think about a super tough day, a lost bid for new work, a poorly done presentation, whatever jumps into your mind. (There's a reason for this—keep reading.)

    Now think about *why* it went the way it did. Be totally honest with yourself. No one is listening. And refrain from the blame game. Were you super stressed? What was distracting you? Were you going through the motions? Was your mind not in the game? Did you not treat someone well? Did you not quality control your work product? Did you lack sleep? You'll know the answer.

Then let it go.

Next, combine your insights from that experience with your findings from the first part of this exercise to focus on your next win. Close your eyes. Imagine your top two ranked distractors are gone. What does winning feel like now? Is it easier? Are you more driven? Are you more present in the moment? Are you excelling? Does the pressure feel lessened? If you're visualizing your next win, the answer to all these questions is *yes*.

Why? Because now you are planning ahead, communicating what you want, limiting involvement with external distractions, ignoring what isn't important, and focusing with all your might on what does matter. You and your business matter. Go for the win.

*Remember, you can excel consistently by focusing on what matters most in the moment.*

## Ask

1. What distracts you most from staying driven to focus on your wins?
2. What can you do for yourself today to dial down the external and internal noise?

## SOLIDIFY WHAT YOU'VE LEARNED

◊ **LESSON 1:** Change course when a new path feels right.

◊ **LESSON 2:** Collect skills and confidence.

◊ **LESSON 3:** Let the strength of kindness flow through you.

◊ **LESSON 4:** Stay driven in the moment to excel under pressure.

## PART THREE
## CONTROL: TAKE CHARGE OF YOUR LIFE

In Part Two, did you gain some clarity on your role in your business and life?

You applied your most useful tool, LTY. You learned how to operate in your performance zone while letting kindness flow through your business, recognizing your knowledge gaps, and transforming some of those gaps into strengths.

Then you positioned yourself to focus to win. The ability to stay driven and present to excel under intense pressure is a challenging feat. Life gets messy, throwing external and internal performance distractions your way. Regardless of whether they are intentional or unintentional, you can LTY.

Practice LTY more and more to develop it into a high-value strength. As you align your business with the real you, you will get to know and appreciate yourself on a deeper level.

Continue reading because you don't want to miss what lies ahead. As you see the sunshine through the clouds, guidance becomes clearer and brighter. The next three chapters explore the theme of emerging as the empowered leader of your life, each showcasing a lesson related to gaining control of the real you. When you carve out space to deal with what you need when you need it, you can finally learn to chill. As a result, you will gain the mind space to look inside yourself to discover more of what makes you unique. Ultimately, you choose the parts of the real you that you want to share with the world.

Let's explore how to live as the real you, starting with carving out space for yourself.

## CHAPTER 5
# CARVE OUT SPACE

Have you ever been blindsided by unpleasant news that changed you in some way?

Life was splendid. I was starting a new global consulting job in New York City. Bigger company. Bigger opportunities. Bigger money.

As part of the onboarding process, I had to go for a mandatory drug screening and physical. No big deal. On a mild, pleasant winter day, I walked from my office to the medical office in my stylish outfit and high heels (in the era of *Sex and the City*, it was a New York thing). I felt blissful.

I dashed into the medical building, assuming I'd be back at the office in no time (billable hours were a professional services thing). I checked in. Shortly thereafter, my name was called. As the exam began, the doctor and I made friendly small talk. Then he started feeling around my neck. His face changed abruptly, and he grew way more serious.

He inquired if I'd ever had my thyroid checked. I said no. "You need to," he stated matter-of-factly. "Sooner rather than later." He explained he felt nodules. Naturally, I asked, "What do you mean?" As I recall, he said something along the lines of it could be nothing, or it could be cancer.

*Shit. You've got to be kidding me,* I thought. As I walked back to the office, the spring in my high-heeled step had disappeared. My legs felt weak. My stomach was knotted. Fear rushed through my veins as chilling thoughts raced through my head. *I just started a new job. How am I supposed to deal with this? Work can't know about this* (yes, that was one of my first thoughts). *Cancer? Did he really say I could have cancer? What if I do have cancer?*

I thought I was going to puke on a New York City sidewalk. This day was no longer splendid.

Months later, after feeling trapped in a medical maze of appointments and tests, I still didn't know if I actually had cancer. How many biopsies did I need to go through to get a definitive answer? I grew to despise the word *indeterminate.*

Finally, after a year of jerking around with an ill-equipped ENT in New Jersey, I took control of my own health. I got my records and scheduled an appointment with a world-renowned, highly recommended head and neck surgeon at Mount Sinai Hospital in New York City.

When I woke up on the morning of my appointment, I was excited. I wanted answers from a skilled, advanced, and innovative doctor. I wanted to know if I had cancer.

There I was in a Mount Sinai waiting room, sitting with some unwell-looking patients. I sat in stillness. However, the quiet brought no rest. I was scared and anxious. After a long wait, I was brought into an exam room.

Despite yet another nerve-wracking wait, I had a powerful, intuitive feeling I was in the right place. When the well-groomed, well-dressed doctor walked in, I noted his gentle eyes and composed demeanor—and they felt magnetic." At that moment, I was confident he was the right specialist to solve my "do I have cancer?" problem. I had retaken control of my health with a compassionate surgeon who finally put me at ease. I had found where I belonged for this part of my health journey.

My biopsy confirmed cancer. Its extent would be unknown until I had surgery. I remember saying something like, "But how? I have no symptoms." Not knowing why I got cancer made it more confusing.

My doctor looked at me and said, "If you are going to have cancer, this is the cancer to have." He tried to steer me toward the realization that I wouldn't *ever* know why. The fact was I had it. He also told me to stay off the internet or I would make myself crazy. He'd already sized me up as the "try to make sense of what you can't make sense of" researcher type. I laughed a bit. He was right.

Any kind of cancer isn't fun. Since the thyroid is one of the body's command centers, I knew I was in for a wild ride. Regardless, during this time, I started using the phrase, "Accept it."

However, "accept it" didn't comfort me when it came to figuring out how work responsibilities fit into my new reality of surgery and cancer treatment. I was so concerned about missing work that I scheduled surgery for the Thursday of Memorial Day weekend so I could miss the fewest possible workdays. At the time, I was running a finance and accounting department. It's not fun telling your boss, colleagues, and team members who rely on you that you must get surgery within months of taking two planned weeks off to go on your honeymoon. I didn't want to let anyone down. (Did I mention I was planning a wedding during all of this?)

Surgery day arrived. The last thing I remember is my trustworthy doctor, with his impeccable bedside manner, warmly telling me everything was going to be okay. He held my hand while telling me to count backward from ten. As I drifted off to sleep, he was elevated to hero healer surgeon status in my mind.

I woke up about six hours later, disoriented and super sick to my stomach, with my husband-to-be Mark by my side. I looked down and saw big clunky boots on my feet. Not exactly *Sex and the City*. A nurse explained I had to wear circulation boots because I'd had a long surgery. I didn't care about my circulation. All I wanted to know was if my thyroid was still in my body and how far my cancer had traveled.

After a couple of hours staring at the ceiling, my surgeon visited me and my space boots. He gently rested his hand on my arm, signaling I was okay without any words. Then he confirmed I no longer had a thyroid. I'd had a complete thyroidectomy. He took care in explaining that he had also taken out some parathyroid glands and lymph nodes, while showing me pictures and the pathology report.

On one hand, I felt relieved that my diseased thyroid was removed by my hero healer. On the other hand, I knew I was in for many more medical visits. My body needed to adjust to not having a thyroid. That entire organ was being replaced with a daily replacement pill. Swapping a pill for an organ that is a critical part of the endocrine system, controlling everything from metabolism to mood, is not as easy breezy as it may sound. Plus, not having four functioning parathyroid glands would affect my body's ability to regulate calcium. This was an added layer to the "you've got to be kidding me" feeling. I kept telling myself, *Accept it*.

On top of all this, I was informed I had to undergo cancer treatment. After digesting this news, I didn't know whether to laugh, cry, or scream.

My incredible doctor advised Mark and I to go be happy newlyweds with a plan to complete the treatment protocol when I got back. The next step would entail radioactive iodine treatment to find and kill any potentially cancerous thyroid tissue remnants post-surgery.

In the meantime, the work didn't slow or stop. I had to keep performing. Although my fiancé and parents didn't get exactly what I was going through, they were by my side as my support system, carrying me through the turbulent waves on strong rafts of love.

Mark and I returned from our honeymoon, and my radioactive iodine treatment plan began within a couple of weeks. The worst part was that I had to stop taking the daily pill for a period for the treatment to be most effective. In retrospect, I would take the surgery part over this process again in a heartbeat. It was absolutely awful.

Within twenty-four hours of not ingesting thyroid medicine when you don't have a thyroid, your body starts a downward spiral. However, I had to last several days without my medicine until my TSH level got high enough to prepare my body for the treatment. I felt and looked like hell. I wanted to crawl into a ball and sleep, growing worse by the hour. I worked anyway.

No thyroid and no thyroid medicine is one of those "you have to live it to fathom it" nightmare situations. Anyone who has been through this understands. Anyone who hasn't, which was everyone around me, doesn't. During this whole ordeal, I dealt with dismissive comments and actions while biting my tongue.

"You look fine."

*Well, I feel like crap.*

"You look good to me."

*Didn't ask you to judge my appearance.*

"Your scar doesn't look so bad."

*I had my neck cut open to remove cancer… do you think I care about my scar? By the way, my hero doctor was a trained plastic surgeon.*

"Are you going to get fat?"

*No, are you?*

"Are you going to be able to have kids?"

*Did you really just ask me that? Yes, idiot, the cancer was in my neck.*

Treatment day arrived on a Friday morning. I couldn't wait to get it done and get on with my life.

What came next was like a strange scene from a movie I never want to see again. At a different hospital, I entered an all-white room where everything, and I mean *everything*, was covered in plastic. No one could enter the room with me. No one warned me about the eeriness of this part. It was something otherworldly. Cold. Scary. Odd.

Next, my treatment doctor entered the room wearing a medical suit of armor carrying a scientific-looking metal container and tongs. Again, I felt like I was watching a movie. Unfortunately, it was real life. My life. She opened the container, then lifted out a pill with her tongs. She dropped this radioactive pill into my palm. Without hesitation, I took the medicine with my plastic cup of water. At that moment, I would have taken anything to make this nightmare end.

I had to stay in this cold, plastic-wrapped room by myself until the radioactive iodine passed through my system, which was estimated to take at least one night. I could only drink water. I was determined to escape this white "prison cell" in twenty-four hours. Since water helped flush the iodine out of my system, I drank as much water as possible as quickly as possible. I drank, drank, drank, and peed, peed, peed. I couldn't sleep that night. Mentally, I needed to get out of that place.

Again, although there was stillness, there was no ease. I had to sit alone with what was real. That reality was me, water, this white, sterile, bubble room, and a bathroom. This discomfort I couldn't escape helped me get comfortable with being present amid chaos.

The next morning, I met my goal by passing the test. The radioactive iodine had left my system. Thankfully, I could go home to our warm, married life. Monday I was back at work.

The next challenging part was waiting for the test results. It was hard to be present. My mind kept wandering to the what-ifs. *What if I still have cancer? What if I have to get another treatment? What if I have to miss more work? What if? What if? What if?*

Fortunately, two agonizing days later, a phone call saved my tired mind from my pessimistic what-if scenarios. In fact, the news was one of the best-case scenarios of my life. The scan showed no remaining cancer. There was a lot to celebrate, including my hero surgeon.

## Reflect

Since this ordeal, I've been cancer free, thanks to finding the right path to healing with the right expert. I will be forever grateful for my talented surgeon and the quality care I received at Mount Sinai Hospital. During this unsettling and unsteady time, a primary lesson pulled me through the darkness (and that white, plastic-wrapped room).

**Persevere with gratitude.**

Although my story ended well, this heavy experience took years to understand in its entirety. It wasn't until after I became a mom that I fully processed my thyroid cancer saga.

The fortitude to persevere during a challenging personal time has the power to help you pass the toughest tests. I wasn't looking to excel. I wasn't looking to get an A. I just wanted to get through it. To survive.

To go a step further, the fortitude to persevere *with gratitude* helps you shut down any pity party. It also gives you the grace to ignore those acting like jerks. When crises happen, it is easy to slip into the "why me, why now?" mode of thinking. It is easy to take to heart the insensitive things some say when you aren't feeling your strongest. It is hard to express gratitude for something that upends your world like a cancer experience does.

Again, why did I select such a personal, vulnerable experience to share? Because the biggest challenges in life affect all aspects of our personal and business lives. Unfortunately, cancer is real. Cancer doesn't care what you do for work, what plans you have, whether you own a business or have a family, where you live, what you look like, how old you are, what kind of clothes or shoes you wear, how much money you make, or what you eat for breakfast.

Cancer blasts into your life announcing, "Here I am. Now, what are you going to do about it?"

Life lessons appear when and how they appear. Hence, my use of the "accept it" mantra. I learned to accept what had happened and my current circumstances; however, I was committed to improving my situation.

As a result of my raw, real, and uncomfortable thyroid cancer saga, I gained strength from realizing I didn't need to know *why* things were the way they were. That night, all alone, the eerie white room gifted to me the private space to accept what was happening to me. And in that space, as my acceptance eased my anxiety, I saw what I had, and I was grateful. My hope of restored health. My family. My future family. Love. Resilience. Even my sanity, although in that stark room, it was certainly being tested.

This lesson has stayed with me professionally and personally. It came from my cancer. And it has come with me to work ever since.

Of course, cancer experience is not required to comprehend this lesson. We have all experienced an unexpected, unwelcome health event or major challenge at some point, whether it happened to us or someone close to us. When we persevere through such physically and mentally trying times, we allow ourselves to accept what is. As we do, we can recognize the good still present in our lives. It is always there; it is just sometimes hidden by resistance and fear. And we can choose to be grateful.

If you can rise to the occasion with gratitude, you give yourself the gift of a perspective that supplies you the power to pull through—to heal. If you don't persist with gratitude, you're choosing to spend your nonrenewable time attending a pity party where you are the guest of honor. Who wants to attend that event?

Let's learn how to align your business and the real you to carve out personal space for yourself to move through unwelcome, unexpected events with grace.

## Learn

When you're in crisis mode, you aren't looking for your most superb performance. You are simply trying to persevere to get through your ordeal. You need to deal with what you need to deal with, when you need to deal with it.

Unwelcome surprises, by definition, pop up unexpectedly in your life. I'm talking about the big, serious ones that get in the way of your work. It could be cancer or something else. It could even be a cluster of unfortunate happenings that cause you to reach your official breaking point.

Then the pity party begins in your mind. It goes something like this.:

*Why me?*
*Why now?*
*How didn't I know?*
*What could I have done differently?*
*How will I get through this?*
*How will I keep working?*
*I don't want to let anyone down.*

## CARVE OUT SPACE

*I can't not work.*
*I feel weak.*
*I want to hide.*
*No one understands.*
*No one gets it.*
*I'm all alone.*

While your mind is occupied in "woe is me" mode, the pile of business pressures and demands continues to grow. Your business and your life don't stop when you encounter a hindrance like a health issue. For example, you're dealing with your unpleasant health news by staying curled up in bed, crying for the second day in a row. Meanwhile, you have half a dozen emails from colleagues and new potential clients wanting to meet with you.

On one hand, internally, your mind is racing and feeling out of control. This is because you feel like your entire life is out of control. On the other hand, externally, you still face real pressures. Your clients, colleagues, and family still need you. They rely on you. You rely on yourself too, which is why you feel so off-kilter and inconvenienced by your life.

As we covered in the last chapter, critical life situations have a way of forcing us to focus. Sometimes you must stay driven to excel no matter what pressure you face.

When crises last longer than a few days, you need more than focus to make it through. You need to carve out space to find the strength to persevere with gratitude. When facing a long-term challenge, during the bleak moments, it's easier to feel down than up. It's easier to feel sorry for yourself than to be grateful. All you feel capable of doing is worrying about the outcomes, thinking about worst-case scenarios, and wondering how you're going to get yourself out of bed that day. As a result, you get yourself into a cycle of think, worry, think, worry. Then you feel worse. You feel more anxious, and you aren't helping yourself. However, you are too consumed by your frantic thoughts to realize it.

When you run a business, how do you forge ahead with gratitude for something that upended your personal life? Well, you focus on what matters most to preserve your mental and physical stamina. *Yeah, sure*, you may think. *Easier said than done.*

The big picture here is that your current crisis is only part of what's transpiring in your life. Naturally, you may feel out-of-sorts. Your workflow may be negatively impacted by your drained energy, low spirits, or time spent at medical appointments. It's okay.

> **You choose which thoughts to keep in your mind and which to escort out of it.**

The key is to understand that internally you choose which thoughts to keep in your mind and which to escort out of it. Externally, you need to carve out space to process what you need to process so you can recenter yourself, see the whole truth about your life (the good and the not-so-good), and persevere with gratitude and grace.

What is the single most valuable tool you own? You guessed it: LTY. Even cancer can't take that away from you. Use it.

LTY will help you persevere through the most trying times to expel debilitating thinking patterns. Then you can find your way around or through the obstacle. Along the way, you also find gratitude and opportunities.

## Apply

You can apply LTY to sense when you need to carve out space for yourself to feel your emotions, accept what is, and gain perspective. When energy and optimism are low, here are five steps to help you find more stamina to persevere with gratitude:

1. **Carve out the space you need.** LTY. If you're noticing your mind is racing with what-if scenarios, negative thoughts, worries, and anxieties, it's time to carve out space. Maybe you feel trapped in a scary, dark medical maze. Maybe you are going down rabbit holes

of internet research about your or your loved one's condition. Maybe you are hiding utter exhaustion along with the shame, weakness, or whatever else you associate with how you really feel. Whatever the case, you need to carve out space for you to deal with what you need to deal with.

Space is needed for different reasons at different times. Sometimes you need space to process news. Sometimes you need space to think or be alone to prepare for what's ahead. Sometimes you need space to heal. And you don't have to tell others more than what they need to know. Space on your terms is an essential human need.

2. **Let yourself come undone.** Now that you carved out the safe space you need, allow yourself to feel whatever you're feeling. You don't need to be a hero. You don't need to wear a coat of armor. Having a good cry privately does not mean you are weak or unstable. It means you are human. During this allotted time, have your pity party. Cry. Scream. Laugh. Stay in bed. Eat ice cream. Do whatever you need to get all those mixed emotions out of your system.

Notice that I said "allotted time." Carving out space is not an open-ended invitation to stay in bed for days, feeling sorry for yourself. You, your business, and your loved ones need you. So give yourself permission to get messy. Then pull yourself together to trek ahead.

3. **Accept the parts you can't change.** You have control over quite a few things in your life, like what you eat for breakfast and when you schedule your first meeting of the day. You do not have control over when something like cancer swoops into your life. Life gets heavy. Life gets hard. Intellectually, you know that worrying does not fix things. In fact, mentally, it makes things worse. What can fix things? When you accept that your current situation is real, you are no longer wasting energy on wishing your life was different. Then you can reallocate those resources to move forward more positively, thinking more clearly about what matters most.

4. **Find your gratitude jewels.** When you accept something you cannot change, that forced need for control naturally dissipates, along

with the angst that accompanies it. Then you can see the whole truth of your life, including the good parts.

Everyone has something to be grateful for. It's on you to find and collect your gratitude jewels. Ask yourself questions such as, What made me smile today? What made me think a happy thought? Who do I enjoy being around? Who makes me feel good? What do I enjoy doing? If I could do anything tomorrow, what would it be? Who would it be with?

You get the idea. Explore thoughts like this to find your gratitude jewels.

5. **Control what you allow in.** Okay, so you have carved out space for yourself, had your pity party, accepted the reality of your situation, and discovered your gratitude jewels. Now comes the hardest part. You control what you allow in your life. Specifically, you can choose to allow what you're grateful for to have a more prominent role in your daily life, no matter what unfortunate circumstances you encounter.

How?

By continuing to accept the reality of your situation.

Now that you've accepted reality, what are you going to do about it? You carve out space for yourself to deal with your personal and business challenges.

What is the biggest hindrance to carving out space for yourself? Allowing yourself to be too accessible.

Ouch. How many of us let ourselves be too accessible? Check our email first thing in the morning? Start responding before we've had a cup of coffee, walked the dog, or exercised? Drop what we're doing to take an impromptu call or meeting? Agree to work calls while on the family vacation we planned months before?

Too many of us, too many times.

Running your own business effectively requires you to be accessible to *you* to focus on your business. A major upside of running your business is you determining when and how to be accessible to your customers, team, network, contacts, and more. A potential client you would like to work with or a consultant you are paying is not going to be offended if you suggest meeting at a mutually convenient time "tomorrow" instead of at 5:30 p.m. today when you want or need to be elsewhere for the good of your business and your life.

You are not in control of everything. But you are in control of more than you realize.

This includes carving out space for yourself to accommodate your needs according to your schedule. Depending on the day, that may be five minutes, an hour or two, or an entire day. If you have to spend a day running to doctors' appointments, then that is what you need to do. You might balance the not-so-enjoyable stuff with things you do enjoy, such as a longer workout, scenic walk outside, nature hike, meal with a friend, or day trip. Or simple things, like a cup of your favorite coffee or extra sleep. No guilt required.

The space you carve out is created by you to be used by you. When you practice doing so, you will be preserving the energy you need to get through your hardest days.

When you add gratitude, your situation feels more doable because you can see that the crisis is not the whole of your life. You feel more connected with what is good in your life. As a result, you feel more confident that you can solve the problems before you.

Let's do some gratitude math, the kind of math you will enjoy.

## Act: The Gratitude Equation

When you're navigating a challenging long-term life event like a health issue or major challenge, it takes dedicated effort and energy to pull yourself through. You can carve out space for yourself to accept what is and free yourself from the unproductive thoughts in your mind. Then you can focus on being grateful for what matters most.

ALIGN YOUR BUSINESS WITH THE REAL YOU

This is no small feat. To accomplish it, here is a tool I call the Gratitude Equation:

**The Gratitude Equation**™

*What Is Real − What Is Not Real +* **Gratitude** = *What Is with Gratitude*

Here are the four steps:

1. **What Is Real:** For this exercise, What Is Real includes what you know to be true about what you are going through. For example, it includes what your pathology report actually says in writing, what your doctor told you directly, or your lab work results. In other words, this is tangible, factually accurate information.
2. **What Is Not Real:** Then subtract What Is Not Real from What Is Real. What Is Not Real (you see it disappearing above) encompasses the countless and torturous scenarios you play in your mind, such as all your doom and gloom, worst-case scenarios, what you imagine others are thinking or saying about your situation, and more. Acknowledge them all, and then let them go. You are removing them from your Gratitude Equation.
3. **Gratitude:** Next, add gratitude. List all the things that are right in your world, as you may have already done in Apply: Step 4. Whatever you are grateful for, feel it, think it, and hold on to it. Imagine you are holding your gratitude jewels in your hands. You want to hold so many that they are spilling over.

    For instance, your gratitude jewels may include your most enjoyable vacation memory, the taste of your favorite food, the sound of your loved one's laughter, an image of playtime with your pets, the scenic sight of a still, blue ocean or white snow-capped mountains, and so on. Envision all the folks who add value to your life because they make you feel good. For example, you may be grateful that your or your loved one's diagnosis was caught early or turned out to be the better-case scenario. You can be grateful for little things like the delicious pancakes you ate at a diner yesterday with your friend. There is no right or wrong answer. Add all that gratitude to What Is Real.

4. **What Is with Gratitude:** You have now taken control of your thoughts about your tough situation. You began with What Is Real, you eliminated What Is Not Real, and you added Gratitude, which equals What Is with Gratitude. You elevated your thoughts to empower yourself to persevere with gratitude.

Recall the Gratitude Equation in your mind whenever you are thrown a curveball you weren't expecting. LTY. The first sign you need to use your Gratitude Equation is when your mind starts wandering into What Is Not Real territory. When this happens, carve out space for yourself to focus on What Is with Gratitude.

*Remember, persevering with gratitude will empower you to push through the toughest challenges and focus on what matters most with grace.*

## Ask

1. Name one significant challenge you're facing that you must persevere through.
2. Think back to the direst event you had to persevere through in the past. How did you make it through? What strengths were revealed? How were you changed for the better?
3. How might your strengths and lessons from your experience help you in your current challenge?

## SOLIDIFY WHAT YOU'VE LEARNED

◊ **LESSON 1:** Change course when a new path feels right.

◊ **LESSON 2:** Collect skills and confidence.

◊ **LESSON 3:** Let the strength of kindness flow through you.

◊ **LESSON 4:** Stay driven in the moment to excel under pressure.

◊ **LESSON 5:** Persevere with gratitude.

## CHAPTER 6
# LEARN TO CHILL

Have you ever reached a dark dead end and then paved your own path toward a new, brighter direction?

One cold February morning I walked my son to elementary school like normal. During the walk home, I also checked my work email—like normal. I read a group email announcing that the company I worked for had been acquired. It was also clear our corporate office would be closing. This was *not* normal.

I knew it was coming, but I didn't know it was coming right then. Despite my senior role at the company, I learned of our company's acquisition in the same note with the typical corporate lingo and explanation that others did.

The first word that came to mind while processing that email was *interesting*. All of a sudden, things said and done that hadn't made sense made total sense. The company had been in a turnaround phase. As a senior leader, I had taken productivity to a whole new level. I worked full weeks, plus I worked from home on weekends. I don't mean an hour here and there; I mean a good chunk of an entire weekend, every weekend. When you're wired to stay focused and excel under pressure, you keep churning out excellence. In turn, some feed on that and give you more and more to do.

It was a vicious cycle that was now over.

As I glanced at the blue sky, the warmth of the sun hit my face. What also hit me in that moment was the sense that my life was changing for the better. I vividly remember looking up at the sky and saying, "Thank you."

That one email marked the end of a significant career chapter of my life. A chapter filled with too much work and not enough resources; too much conflict and not enough collaboration; too much expectation and not enough gratitude; too much pretense and not enough truth.

However, nothing that preceded that email mattered anymore. The deal was done. In a way, my ability to produce quality results quickly worked me out of a job even faster. The irony of it all was not lost on me. So off I went to work that day, knowing my career train stop had arrived. I wasn't moving to another state. I would accept my package and go my own way. I thought, *Accept it, move on.*

The odd vibe throughout the office was palpable. Understandably so. The New Jersey office would be closing. I simply observed certain occurrences with the word *interesting* on repeat in my mind. One thing I had mastered by this point in my career was the power of silence.

Starting that day, I did some things the same and some things differently, all while showing up every day as a professional persevering through an awkward situation with gratitude. I walked my son to school every day, now at a more relaxed pace. However, during the walk home, I no longer walked with my head down, looking at my phone to check my work email. I enjoyed the time outside as I looked up and around.

One day in March, I observed birds chirping because I was present enough to hear the sounds around me. Had my life become so hectic that I had stopped noticing birds chirping? *Yes.* The birds were telling me to wake the F up! At least, that was my translation of the powerful message I was receiving. Message received.

Those brilliant birds symbolized the start of a profound personal growth period in my life. I was on a new path.

That day at work, I reclaimed my life. No one would control me but me. I began stepping outside during lunchtime to breathe some fresh

# LEARN TO CHILL

air. Now that's a concept: fresh air during my workday! I also left the office on time every night, leaving work behind. Completely behind.

As the days went on, I continued to preserve my time, energy, and mental space. I cooked fresh meals again during the week. We ate dinner at a decent hour as a family. I caught up on medical appointments. I volunteered more. I spent valuable time with our aging dog, Roxy, and my parents.

As I carved out more space for myself and my family, I felt more anchored to what mattered most. I scheduled family outings, vacations, and visits with friends. I slept better. I woke up more energized. The best part was that my family and I enjoyed our weekends together. The vibe in our home was more peaceful. I was more peaceful.

Outside of our home, my news was met with a mix of judgment, questions, and opinions. I fielded comments, including the following, while once again holding my tongue:

"Oh, I'm so sorry, you lost your job."

*I'm not.*

"Well, you got laid off (implying they had something I didn't)."

*What's your point?*

"You should have another baby."

*You should mind your own business.*

"You look so happy (while looking at me with judgment)."

*You say that like it's a bad thing.*

"You can afford to be home. You only have one kid."

*Did I ask your opinion?*

"You don't have another job yet?"

"No, I'm choosing to enjoy my life right now (with an ear-to-ear grin)." This response I actually said, and it left them speechless every time.

In April, the pace of my awakening quickened. My approaching last day combined with folks not knowing when to zip it revealed the last of what I hadn't yet learned from my thyroid cancer journey. Finally, it clicked. My current mission was to figure out how to chill. That became my focus. This quest made going to work for the next two months easier. I was more at ease because I knew what I needed to do to support myself.

My final day in June arrived. I woke up more vivacious than I had been in years. As I walked into my barren office, sitting on my empty desk was a beautiful arrangement of pink peonies. They were a thoughtful gift from an exceptional member of my team who knew pink peonies were my favorite flower—and why. Happy tears filled my eyes and a sweet hug followed.

By 1:00, I handed in my computer, signed formalities, cradled my beautiful pink peonies, and exited the building. I got into my car, turned on my playlist curated for the occasion, opened the sunroof, and drove away from the work world I had been living in. I didn't belong there anymore.

My husband was waiting for me at home. We enjoyed a relaxing outdoor lunch, which felt heavenly. Then I sat outside bathing in the sun's rays and their vitamin D, while chatting with one of my close friends who knew the whole work saga. The best part was seeing our son's smiling face after school that day.

Intentionally, I had no job lined up. I was learning to chill.

I didn't know where I was heading. However, I knew it was going to be wonderful. At last, I was free to fly like the birds.

## Reflect

The end of this career phase was set in motion by a company sale. However, the priceless knowledge I collected about myself and what I needed to do next was set in motion by me. At this point, I was seeing things as I saw them instead of how others thought I needed to see them, or how they wanted me to see them. I started to make decisions based on what I wanted to do.

Similar to my thyroid cancer journey, I gained strength from accepting actual circumstances. I was grateful for my full life outside of my career. The difference was that I was no longer fixated on work or my career. I didn't need to know where and when my next job would be. I took an intentional break to focus on myself and my family. Once I slowed down my pace enough to be more present, the lesson embedded in this experience became apparent.

**Redefine what accessibility means to you.**

We know what accessibility literally means. However, most of us could redefine what accessibility means in terms of the quality of our own lives. We need to shake things up—or have things shaken up for us.

It is easy to bury parts of our real selves when we're constantly trying to please others. If we let external judgments, questions, and opinions affect our thinking and actions, we can get distracted. While we're satisfying others, working constantly, worrying, ruminating, and whatever else, we're not present. We're not even accessible to ourselves.

Amid these thoughts, I further realized that accessibility is impacted by how we define productivity. Productivity doesn't have to mean we are always doing. I learned to move away from productivity toward *prioritization*. Prioritization means we are thoughtfully allocating time to capture the most value. Sometimes the best creativity or bursts of activity come after we prioritize taking a break, even if it's merely a few minutes of fresh air.

Why did I share this story? Because it is a real-life example of how you can lose something because you need to lose it. You may choose to leave something behind, or others may make the choice for you. It doesn't matter. The result is the same. You needed to be freed of what was holding you back to drive your life forward toward the destination you have chosen.

Although this lesson was learned during a career transition, it is one I call upon regularly in any context. It helps me be more accessible to what matters most and inaccessible to what truly doesn't matter.

> **If you learn from what seems like a loss, you win what's yours and lose what wasn't meant to be yours.**

You don't have to lose a job to learn this lesson. We have all experienced some sort of transition that ultimately helped us figure out what we need and what we really want. If you learn from what seems like a loss, you win what's yours and lose what wasn't meant to be yours.

When you redefine what accessibility means to you, you recover your impressive ability to take control of your life. And when you recover your ability to take control, you can shift your reality. After all, you're the one living your life.

Your ability to chill is a skill that can emerge as a strength. Taking control of your accessibility is a huge leap forward in shaping a more fulfilling life. Let's learn how to redefine *your* accessibility.

## Learn

Speed and business tend to go hand in hand. Each month is a sprint, then each quarter becomes a sprint, and then each year becomes a sprint. Figuratively, your legs are worn out. They need to learn to walk again.

Stress and business ownership also tend to go hand in hand. Put it all together and you are creating a cycle of running your business while pushing and pulling yourself to unhealthy limits.

In the last chapter, we explored tactics for dealing with the big stuff that unexpectedly affects your life. Here, we're exploring how to navigate the "normal" flow of life that ends up influencing your accessibility, which can affect the way you live in a big way.

When you're programmed to go, go, go, faster, harder, higher, eventually you forget how to chill. When you reach this point, you have less time for what and who makes you happy, no time for yourself, and an abundance of stress. You may even look around you to find nosy, gossipy, jealous, judgmental, mean-spirited, or unfiltered folks (or all of the above) in your orbit. These are red flags signaling you are in dire need of a timeout. You say things to yourself like this:

# LEARN TO CHILL

*Sure, I can do that too.*
*Why did I agree to this?*
*Did they really just say that to me?*
*Why would they act that way toward me?*
*I feel like I'm going through the motions.*
*I work way too much.*
*I'm always running from one thing to the next.*
*I have no time for myself.*
*I don't have a safe space.*
*I feel stressed all the time.*
*I don't feel well.*

When you have a business to run, you feel pressure to keep running. Your intentions are good—but who are you running with? Where are you running to? Do you even know why you are running? Is running making you feel happier or painfully fatigued? Are you present enough to realize how fast you're running? Do you even *like* running so much?

As you learned in Chapter 4, during short-term crises, being focused to win fuels you to stay driven to excel, no matter what pressure you face.

And as you learned in Chapter 5, when you're experiencing long-term challenges, you need to carve out space to find the strength to persevere with gratitude. Now, we are talking about recognizing the need to stop running on fumes. We are talking about learning to chill to refuel, re-energize, re-engage, and refocus.

When you're running around to run your business, it's easy to agree to squeeze in another client, attend another meeting, speak at an event, take on more projects, volunteer for another charity, travel to a conference, and more. That one moment, when it seemed easiest and fastest to say yes, ends up creating long strings of moments that will entangle you far into the future.

As a result, you're more and more stressed and less and less present. You wake up during the night thinking it might be a good idea to get up and start working because you have two days' worth of work to squeeze into one. And that's only the business part of your life.

On the personal side, you're also running around to take care of your home, family, and maybe pets. While you're doing all this, are you enjoying yourself? Are you hearing the birds chirp when you walk the dog? Or are you rushing to walk the dog, wanting them to do their thing so you can run off to work? Do you enjoy your workout, or has it gotten to the point where it feels like another thing to check off your to-do list? Do you even enjoy the party you RSVPd yes to because you dread conversing with the unfiltered person who asks you too many personal questions?

*Who has time to listen to the birds chirping?* you may be thinking. Well, if you don't hear the birds chirping, no one can make you hear them. Your ability to chill resides in your commitment to chill.

If you've been running around to run your life, your solution is *redefining your accessibility*. Only you have the power to define your accessibility. In the last chapter, you started to think about over accessibility as a barrier to carving out space for yourself to deal with your personal and business challenges. Now you're going to focus on overcoming this barrier for good. And you don't learn to chill by booking a vacation. You learn to chill in each moment of your daily life.

How? First, know you can control how much you chill. *Yes, you can.* Second, rethink who and what gets access to you, starting with giving yourself an all-access pass. *Yes, you can.* Call upon your most valuable tool: LTY. It will help you uncover what accessibility means to you and why it matters.

## Apply

When you become used to constantly doing, the bar keeps rising. This is fine in some parts of your life. However, when you sense the real you is being gobbled up by your calendar, commitments, and folks around you who don't truly support you, here are four ways to help you find more calmness, less inner turmoil:

1. **Decide how you want to allocate your time.** LTY. For now, put productivity to the side. Don't think in terms of billable hours, fees, revenue, or profits. Don't focus on how much you can accomplish in a day. Don't think about how you need to be productive to make money. We'll get to that in Part Five. Instead, focus on how you *want* to allocate your time while running your business. How do you want to reconfigure your time allocations to lead your business and your life effectively?

   You have far more control than you realize. It's time to tap into it. Start by allocating general blocks of time to important activities. Although business ownership commonly leads to a fuzzy line between your work and personal lives, here you are going to start drawing some protected areas.

   First, start with three: work, personal, sleep.

   | Work | Personal | Sleep |

   Allocate the amount of time you want for each of these general areas. Yes, you are allocating time to sleep. If you aren't sleeping well, you aren't living well. You can frame out different schedules for different days. That's up to you.

   Then, divide the work and personal areas into specific categories that are most important to you. For instance, work categories can include client work, team development, business development, events, networking, travel time, speaking engagements, and administration. Personal categories include chill time, exercise, errands, appointments, family activities, household chores, and more. Allocate the amount of time you want for each of these more specific areas as well.

   If you don't map out how you truly want to allocate your time, you won't get there.

2. **Prioritize how you allocate your time.** Now that you have identified the work, personal, and sleep areas you need to accommodate, prioritize how you allocate your time. Yes, you will need to flex to

accommodate things that pop up unexpectedly. That's okay. Accept it. Prioritize your time in general terms.

Let's explore how you might prioritize the basics: client work, personal activities, exercise, and household chores.

Typically, client work and work that attracts more clients is a priority for business owners. This gets tricky when client responsibilities become so demanding that other tasks and activities in your life take a back seat, including your sleep.

For example, you squeeze in another client to a fully booked day when you know you want to make it to a non-work event early that evening. You know the likely outcome. Yet, you serve the client first anyway—and you miss the event that was important to you. Are you happy about it? No. How do you get happier? You prioritize what you want to do.

When you own a business, you can prioritize personal activities in a way that makes sense for you. Take hold of your calendar. *Yes, you can.* Schedule the doctor appointments. Take care of things you've been putting off. Acknowledge that some days, family needs will take precedence over work and vice versa. It's okay.

Exercise, like sleep, deserves space on your calendar. What's the point of running your business if you're not taking care of the physical body that makes all this running possible? Figure out what time of day works for you to exercise. *Yes, you can.*

Besides all this, you will be well-served to prioritize your household chores. Let's talk about laundry. Why laundry? Because it's an easy, necessary task with a beginning, middle, and end that can be a total time suck. Who wants to spend free hours on a weekend doing laundry? How do you prioritize this? Well, it doesn't belong at the top of your list. However, if it falls to the bottom, you will end up spending a chunk of time climbing out of your dirty laundry mound. You can commit to do some on certain days or each day so it doesn't pile up by the weekend. Do the same with other household responsibilities. You can reduce stress by not letting them pile up. Do them regularly or delegate them. You get the idea.

3. **Revise who you grant access to you.** You also have control over who gets access to you. View yourself as a precious resource for yourself and those who truly love and support you within a self-created safe space.

   To simplify how to decide who gets access to your time and energy, think of access in terms of all access (A), limited access (L), and denied access (D), or what I call the ALD approach. For example, the family members who love and support you unconditionally get an all-access pass (A). Deny access to the time wasters like random sales folks who email and call, wanting time on your calendar, or the frenemy who was never really your friend in the first place (D). Colleagues and customers get limited access (L).

   When you run a business, how can you turn away from potential connections when you want to grow your business? You're not. You can grant them limited access as you see fit. You're turning toward what aligns with the real you and letting in who makes sense for where you are and where you want to go.

   ○ ◐ ●™
   *ALD*

4. **Set your level of personal privacy.** The ALD access approach will help you keep your inner life personal. Your personal life is for you. You're the one living it.

   Folks may think they are entitled to ask you personal questions, pass judgments, or tell you what you should do. They aren't. No one gets to "should on" you. Take back all your control in this facet of your life right now. You don't have to answer everyone's questions. You don't have to spend a second thinking about what others think about you. You also don't have to go out of your way to keep individuals in your orbit who don't add some sort of collaborative happiness, contentment, or other quality to your life. Access denied.

   You also get to choose how much you share publicly about your personal life. This is a decision influenced by your personality. For example, some may love sharing a lot about their personal lives, while others share with only a select few. Your personal and business moves do not need to be on social media. You decide what and when you want to share.

Your responsibilities and priorities will shift with the ebbs and flows of life. Be flexible as long as your level of accessibility is working for you. What does not change is that you are the one who determines your priorities.

Redefining your accessibility is essential for stress management. Now, let's practice a good kind of silence.

## Act: The Silence Solution

As you redefine your accessibility, you can use what I call the Silence Solution as a tool to preserve your personal space as needed. The Silence Solution will enhance your chill time.

Here are the two simple steps to find peace in silence:

1. **Adjust your calendar.** First, prioritize regular time to be *alone* in silence. This is not the time to work out, do work, read email, or check social media. This is time you will spend with yourself in silence. For example, you can meditate, take a walk outside, or sit alone (pets are allowed) to gather your thoughts for the day.

    When would you most benefit from this time? Is it first thing in the morning before your house wakes up? Is it mid-afternoon when you start to feel the work pile on? Is it before the dinner time chaos? Is it at night, right before you drift off to sleep? If spending time in silence is not part of your regular practice, start with at least one optimal time slot for an increment of at least ten minutes twice per week. *Yes, you can.*

Next, block out the time on your calendar and set an alarm on your phone to hold you accountable. Play around with the time slots and length of time. When you find ones that work, build up to five days per week, then daily. Give the results time to kick in. Once you feel your daily mood and energy improve, you will want to commit to your chill time. You will start to crave it. Ask me how I know.

2. **Adjust your reaction to others.** For this one, think about the most recent infringements on your personal space. For example, it might be the person who constantly wants from you, the filterless person who asks you nosy questions, the terse text message you received from someone who didn't have the temerity to pick up the phone, or the so-called friend or colleague who bad mouths you when you're not around (but they act nice to your face). The specific list of unnecessary energy-zapping exchanges will be unique for every individual, but we all have them.

None of them matter. You are in control of how you respond to each and every occurrence. And you can choose to respond in silence. A snippy text message doesn't earn a response. You don't owe nosy types answers about your life to give them fresh material for their gossip cliques. Those who talk badly behind your back don't get any more of your time or energy. No, no, and no. Sometimes, silence is the best and only answer.

Use this two-part Silence Solution whenever you need to create space for yourself or establish a limit. LTY. Repeat the steps as often as needed. Tweak as you go. Let silence be part of your solution to stress.

The Silence Solution may leave a few folks perplexed. That's okay. As long as you apply these strategies with kindness, you aren't doing anything wrong. In fact, your silence is speaking volumes about how you're owning what is yours, including your respect and self-worth.

*Remember, redefining what accessibility means to you will help you decide what and who occupies your sacred physical, emotional, and mental space.*

## Ask

1. Can you think of a time in your life when you lost something significant, and that loss created space for something more fulfilling? Did you set this change in motion, or was it decided for you?
2. Before you read this chapter, what did accessibility mean to you? Now what does it mean? Did your view of accessibility change? If so, how?

## SOLIDIFY WHAT YOU'VE LEARNED

◊ **LESSON 1:** Change course when a new path feels right.

◊ **LESSON 2:** Collect skills and confidence.

◊ **LESSON 3:** Let the strength of kindness flow through you.

◊ **LESSON 4:** Stay driven in the moment to excel under pressure.

◊ **LESSON 5:** Persevere with gratitude.

◊ **LESSON 6:** Redefine what accessibility means to you.

## CHAPTER 7
# LOOK INSIDE

Has someone ever asked you a question that revealed to you something important about yourself?

One afternoon, I was going through my closet with a friend who was helping me prepare for an event. I wanted to wear something vibrant.

"Don't you have any pink?" she asked.

I flipped through some blouses and dresses. The closest option I had was a silky champagne blouse, but in this case, the champagne was not pink. "No," I responded, surprised.

After concluding I had some shopping to do, I went about my day. However, that question, "Don't you have any pink?" kept playing back in my mind in an unsettling way. I believed this question was guiding me toward more awareness about myself, but I wasn't sure what I needed to see.

That night, I sauntered upstairs to spend some quality personal time with my closet. As I perused the array of sweaters, blouses, jackets, pants, skirts, and shoes, I saw a sea of blue, navy, black, olive, gray, white, and beige, with a few pops of bright colors like red. No pink.

As a little girl, I dressed my Barbie dolls in pink. I gladly wore pink in dance recitals. As a teenager, my bedroom was pink. And in my closet back then, there was plenty of pink.

Today, I love colorful flowers, especially pink peonies. Why don't I wear pink now? *I wear pink nail polish*, I thought, to make myself feel better. *I wear pink lipstick. Does that count?*

I knew the answer. *Nice try. No.*

Closets house more than clothes and shoes. They hold glimpses into our personality, style, and mindset. In the language of fashion, they tell a version of the current story of our lives. There was a reason Carrie Bradshaw's closet played a role in *Sex and the City*. It reflected her life.

During this impromptu, somewhat disturbing journey through my closets, past and present, I uncovered some of what I needed to see. I was staring right at it. Although classic, my clothing choices had become limited to black, navy, gray, and beige. This reflection of me was too *blah*. It didn't feel like me.

Why?

Part of the reason was the era in which I entered the New York City finance world. Walking the streets near high-rise office buildings during rush hour or lunch, I saw a sea of blue. Racing around Penn Station or Port Authority in the morning or evening, I noticed professionals wearing darker colors. Let's face it, navy and black are timeless business clothing colors, especially in New York City.

I'll never forget my first high-end "power suit." It was a classic navy vertical pinstripe Armani pant suit I bought at Saks Fifth Avenue. I remember having it tailored to perfection. I remember picking it up at Saks in a nice garment bag, carrying it out of the store with a confident, happy spring in my step. I remember being excited about debuting it at a client meeting. That suit traveled wrinkle free to Paris and London. I loved every inch of it. It was an outstanding, strong, and timeless representation of me for that place, at that time.

Another part of the reason was my personality. Then or now, I probably would not arrive at a business meeting from New Jersey in London or Paris wearing a pink suit. Although my fashion sense wasn't loud or daring, now that I had left the corporate world, I could certainly show up wearing more than pink nail polish or lipstick.

I needed to sit down and chill with my closet for more revelations.

I'd be there a while longer. Pink champagne would have been good right about then.

While I pondered my fashion life journey, I took a shoe detour. I tried on some of my favorite shoes to cheer me up. Pretty shoes always lightened my mood, like my gunmetal Jimmy Choo stilettos I wore to the Tribeca Film Festival years before. I recalled the outfit I wore that night. Guess what color it was? Black.

I smiled. *Next time I wear these shoes, they will be paired with bright colors*, I thought.

I had collected shoes that told stories I had never pieced together until now. Sexy shoes. Confident shoes. Red-soled shoes. Commuting shoes. Flat shoes. Wedding shoes. Honeymoon shoes. Summer shoes. Fashion sneakers. Workout sneakers.

Although some had color, none were pink.

Pink issues aside, my shoes reflected the story of starting out in the big city, "making it" in the city, becoming a mom, moving into the corporate world, leaving where I didn't belong, and now being a career-minded woman in a different phase of motherhood, figuring out how to balance my aspirations with what matters most to me. At this point, I realized my clothing and shoe choices reflected my career progression, personality, and practicality. And that was okay. I love walking my dogs in cute sneakers.

What was *not* okay was that I still didn't know the answer to *Why no pink?*

I was determined to solve this *that night*. So I listened to myself. As I dug further inside my closet, I dug further inside myself. My dog Roxy watched me with a quizzical look in her pretty brown, almond-shaped eyes.

I unearthed a few treasures buried in my closet, like an article of memorabilia from an unforgettable rock concert. I hadn't brought that part of me to work in a long time. Although I had listened to music in my office, I played it at such a low volume that no one could hear it. No one would have known that I enjoyed a wide range of music, or that in the summer, I like to listen to country.

Around midnight, I finally uncovered what I needed to see. The way I showed up reflected my environment more than it reflected myself. In that moment, I sighed with a mix of relief and realization. Roxy perked her head up. I hadn't become drab. I had dimmed myself to match my drab environment. Of course I had been reaching for dark instead of light, mundane instead of vibrant. Of course I had been keeping the volume turned down at work. Fashion and music are outward reflections of how we feel.

Heavy stuff. None of that mattered anymore. I was no longer in that environment. I was taking charge of my life. I was free to choose my environment *and* how I would show up. I could arrive as I wanted, as myself.

The next day, I shopped for pink.

## Reflect

My closet journey unfolded from the simple question, "Don't you have any pink?" Because I had learned to listen to myself, use my strengths, and chill, I was present enough to look inside both my closet and myself that night. I found more than I expected. I discovered a life lesson.

**Choose to show up as the real you.**

Why did I share this story? Because it is a somewhat lighthearted illustration of the importance of examining yourself. When this lesson showed up for me, I was navigating an internal evolution. My career changed. As a result, my tastes in what I wore, what I ate, who I spent time with, and what topics I talked about were changing. I was changing.

Some passing moments lead to lasting outcomes. Since that night, I have filled many large bags with clothing donations for Goodwill. I made room in my closet for lively shades of pink, blue, and green.

And this lesson helped me clean out more than just my closet. It allowed me to clear mental space to allow myself to be who I wanted to be. I was coming alive in color and sound, living my life loud and clear.

I craved levity and laughter *during* my workday. To this day, this lesson reminds me to check in regularly with the outer and inner layers of myself to make sure they're aligned with each other and who I want to be.

To learn this lesson, you don't have to look inside your closet. Fashion is one surface layer of a comprehensive you. The real you runs deeper than your clothing and career choices. This is about how you want to live in *all* your layers and making sure all the layers are in alignment. While your self-expressive outer layers might include fashion, career, music, or cars, your deeper, inner layers include how you want to spend your time, who you want to share your time with, what you enjoy talking about, what you choose to listen to, and how you value friends and family.

It's easy to let the real you slip away unintentionally as you assimilate more and more to your environment. As you're buried in work and demands, you keep going like a wind-up doll. Add to that trying to please others and satisfy their needs. Before long, you're solely focused on your environment. You lose a sense of the real you.

When you hit pause, you can start asking yourself questions about what showing up as the real you means to you. Then, you empower yourself as the designer of your life. The outward and inward you are being led by *you*.

Choosing to be the best, genuine version of yourself is another step toward living a life that feels good for you. Let's look at how you can live more as the real you in all your environments.

## Learn

Leading your own business takes focus and energy, no doubt. You run and run more, do and do more, give and give more.

Tending to non-work areas of your life also takes focus and energy. Now, you run even more, do even more, and give even more.

This is all normal. There is an upside. There is a downside.

In the last chapter, we explored how to navigate the flow of life by controlling your accessibility. It's important to train yourself to stop running and start chilling. When you give yourself a regular "timeout" amid everyday moments, you can view things from a clearer perspective.

Now, we are acknowledging the need to check in with yourself by taking a look *inside* yourself. Here we are only focused on *you*.

In your haste to get things done, it's easy to lose focus on yourself as a human being separate from your business, separate from your family, separate from the rest of your life. When the pace of your everyday life moves so fast, it's easy to leave parts of you behind.

Also, changing is a natural part of life. You grow. You mature. You improve. Your tastes in what you eat, what you wear, who you hang out with, what you talk about, and how you live daily life shift over time. That's why it's imperative to regularly check in with yourself. As entrepreneurial leaders, you are wired to search more, ask why, reassess now, improve faster, create change, and share lessons with those who listen and learn, so they, too, can do the same. If you are evolving as leaders, the person you were yesterday may not be who you are today or will be in the future. That's okay.

However, it's not okay when you lose so much of yourself that you don't even realize it's happening. It's easy to get sucked into external validation mode, thinking you need to do, say, or be this or that, to receive someone else's acceptance, recommendation, or praise. It's easier to fit in when you blend in.

Next thing you know, the path of least resistance led you to somewhere you didn't intend to go. You've changed. And you may not even realize it.

How can you show up as the real you when you're not sure who the real you is? Have the self-awareness and courage to look inside yourself.

This is where a personal check-in will serve you well. A personal check-in is simply a question-and-answer session with yourself, about yourself. It can go something like this:

*How do I feel?*
*How do I really feel?*

*Do I feel healthy?*
*Do I feel happy?*
*Am I taking care of myself?*
*How do I look?*
*How do I really look?*
*Does my work fulfill me?*
*Do I feel engaged?*
*Who do I enjoy being around the most?*
*What customers do I enjoy serving?*
*What do I enjoy doing in my free time?*
*What do I enjoy talking about?*
*What do I do to relax?*
*What do I crave?*
*What do I need to let go?*

You may be thinking, *Who has time to hold a question-and-answer session with themselves?* No one can force you to do this. No one can do it for you. Your ability to show up as the real you relies on you *knowing* the real you.

> **You have an all-access pass to yourself. Use it.**

At the same time, prioritizing personal check-ins isn't easy. If you're not used to this kind of internally focused practice, it may feel uncomfortable. It's possible you're afraid of what you will find.

That's okay. Only you are examining you. No one is listening. No one is watching. No one is judging. You have an all-access pass to yourself. Use it.

Once you gain an understanding of your inner workings, you gain hold of *all* of you. You accept the you that you are today. You figure out what is most important to you. You decide what parts of your true being you want to share with others.

As a business owner, the parts you share with the world are up to you. You control what you wear, what you talk about, who you are surrounded by, how you spend your time. Do you want to laugh more at work? Do you want to add levity to meetings? Do you want to talk about your kids more in the workplace? Do you want to avoid political discussions? Do you want to listen to your favorite music? Do you want to wear pink? You get the idea.

You have arrived at a point in your life when you have earned the courage and confidence to walk into a room as the real you. It's time to start living your life in color.

As always, when you check in with yourself, call upon your most valuable tool: LTY. It will guide you toward your truest sense of self.

## Apply

When you start to feel a disconnect between how you show up and how you *want* to show up, take a look inside you (and perhaps your closet).

Here are four steps to help you look inside and choose to show up as the real you:

1. **Accept where you are right now.** Whatever is going on, wherever you are, accept it. Surrender to experience inner peace and the best version of you.

    If you feel stressed and exhausted, you may not look so good because you don't feel so well. Your low energy or mood may have you reaching for "easy" clothes to wear that don't flatter you. If you peek into your closet or drawers, you may be staring at a disarray of clothes that doesn't reflect the best version of yourself. It's okay. Don't judge yourself.
2. **Look at the external you.** Now, take a good look at yourself. This is not an invitation to be harsh with yourself. Even the most gorgeous people in the world have fat, ugly, and stupid days. Be gentle with yourself. You are unique, beautiful, and special.

    Now ask yourself some questions with kindness and curiosity. Do you wear your favorite, feel-good colors? Are you holding onto things that no longer serve you? Does what you wear reflect the current version of you, or better yet, the version you want to be?

Fashion is much more than clothes, accessories, trends, and brands. How you *feel* in what you wear provides the outside world, and your own reflection, a glimpse into your state of mind.

Therefore, think about how other aspects of you show up externally. For example, what attitude do you display throughout your day? What do your facial expressions say? Do you smile?

Also, look at the spaces in which you function, including your home, workspaces, and car. If you own a car that you drive frequently, observe the inside. Is it neat or messy? Is your workplace orderly or disorganized? Is your home tidy or cluttered? Any of those observations could be telling you something.

3. **Look at the internal you.** Now look deeper. What's your inside story?

The easiest, most direct way to capture the inner parts of the real you is to explore focused questions:

- How did your childhood influence you as an adult?
- What and who do you value the most in your life?
- What brings out your inner confidence?
- What is your favorite time of day to think clearly?
- What motivates you to get stuff done at work or around the house?
- What are your tastes in music? Do you like to listen to certain music when you exercise, walk, drive, or think? Do your music tastes change with the seasons or with your tasks? There's no right or wrong answer here.
- What are your favorite foods? Do you opt for salty or sweet? What is your favorite ice cream flavor?
- What types of books do you read? What podcasts and radio shows do you listen to regularly? Are you a physical turn-the-page reader, ebook reader, or audiobook listener?
- What shows or movies capture your attention?

- What hobbies and non-work activities interest you?
- Where and how do you like to chill?
- Where did you go on your last vacation? What was your most memorable vacation? Where do you want to travel to next?
- Do you own pets? How do they brighten your day?
- Do you like talking about your family during your workday? Or are you all about work during your workday?
- What topics come naturally to you when you're networking or with colleagues?

Add any other questions that help you capture the real you. And don't forget to ask yourself why you answered the way you did. Dive deeper to gain more information about yourself.

> **You can get stuff done while looking and feeling confident and happy.**

4. **Visualize your desired self.** Now you get to design your desired self. And I don't mean dreaming of a hotter body or a closet full of Chanel or Burberry runway looks.

   During this step, take the information you downloaded from steps two and three, digest it, and decide how you want to enter any business encounter or situation as the *real* you.

   First, look at the external. How do you want to appear? What types of clothes are you wearing (within your budget)? Are you composed? Are you wearing a smile? You *can* get stuff done while looking and feeling confident and happy. If you want to wear hot pink shoes to a virtual meeting because it makes you feel cheerful, go ahead.

   Are you signaling gentleness with colleagues and acquaintances, with pleasantries like "good morning," "did you have a nice weekend/holiday?" "safe travels," or "have a nice evening"?

   Are you doing things that raise your energy, like activities you enjoy or trying something new with friends, family, or colleagues who make you feel good? Are you laughing during your waking hours? If you aren't laughing, you aren't living your best life.

And perhaps the most important part of your desired self: Do you feel content, healthy, fulfilled, and valued?

If you're daydreaming right now with images of your best self, good for you. Now, come back to the key takeaways.

*You choose how you show up as the real you.* The real you who deserves to laugh and smile during the workday. The real you who gets stuff done while looking and feeling confident and happy. The real you who acknowledges that some of your tastes and desires will shift with the natural unfolding of life.

Keep checking in with yourself. You don't need to change who you really are to be where you are if it's where you fundamentally belong.

Now, let's create something unique for you to share with others.

## Act: The Five-Layer Cake

After completing the above four steps to help you choose to show up as the real you, you are ready to bring the real you to wherever you are. To do so, you can share the "Five-Layer Cake," created, mixed, baked, and assembled to perfection by you. The five layers represent aspects of yourself that you want to share with the world. Private aspects of your life that you don't intend to share are not baked into the cake.

You get to choose how you will craft your cake combination. No shopping, oven, or calories required. Be creative as you compile all the layers of the real you.

Here are the five layers from bottom to top:

## ALIGN YOUR BUSINESS WITH THE REAL YOU

*(Cake diagram: personality (cherry on top), How, Where, When, What, Who)*

- **Layer 1: Who.** Who do you enjoy spending time with? (Pets count.) Who makes you feel valued? Who makes you feel happiest?

    The "who" comes first because these are the ones you want to be sure to share your cake with and spend more time with.

- **Layer 2: What.** What do you do for work? What do you do for fun? What topics do you like talking about? What are your hobbies and interests? What music do you listen to? What sports do you follow? What shows do you watch? What books do you read? What makes you laugh?

    Share these things with others at a meeting, event, dinner, or other public setting.

- **Layer 3: When.** When do you feel your best? When do you do your clearest thinking? When do you look your best? When do you smile most?

    This layer helps you show up clear minded, engaged, and looking and feeling fabulous.

- **Layer 4: Where.** Where are your favorite spots to think, work, play, dine, rest? Where do you like to go for fun? Where do you go to relax? Where do you feel the most comfortable?

    Frequent these places more. It's easier to walk in a room smiling and shining when you are where you want to be.

- **Layer 5: How.** How are you unique? How do you want to project the real you? How do you bring kindness as a strength? How much do you smile and laugh during your workday? How do you chill?

Visualize the inner you shining through the outer you. Bring the you that radiates your good vibes to others.

- **Icing, Sprinkles, and a Cherry on Top: Personality.** What's your style? How do you show up externally? What comprises the external layer of your personality that others see?

When you bring your cake to a party, this is what others see first. As you put the finishing touches on your cake, think of the icing as the fashion styles and colors you choose. Sprinkles symbolize your ability to add levity, laughter, and love to any room. Finally, the cherry on top is the smile that speaks volumes in any room, in any situation.

Keep in mind that the Five-Layer Cake you bake today may not be the same cake you make six months or a year or three years from now. The flavors of your layers may change as you evolve. For example, your "What" layer could change as your business morphs into something else or your interests or tastes shift. That's all okay.

Repeat this exercise as often as you want to bake new cakes that reflect the current version of you.

*Remember, showing up as the real you will empower you to live the life you want in full color.*

## Ask

1. Can you think of a time in your life when a passing moment led to a lasting, beneficial outcome for you? How did the outcome unfold for you?
2. Before you read this chapter, what did "showing up as the real you" mean to you? Now what does it mean to you? What did you learn that will impact the way you show up?

## SOLIDIFY WHAT YOU'VE LEARNED

◊ **LESSON 1:** Change course when a new path feels right.

◊ **LESSON 2:** Collect skills and confidence.

◊ **LESSON 3:** Let the strength of kindness flow through you.

◊ **LESSON 4:** Stay driven in the moment to excel under pressure.

◊ **LESSON 5:** Persevere with gratitude.

◊ **LESSON 6:** Redefine what accessibility means to you.

◊ **LESSON 7:** Choose to show up as the real you.

# PART FOUR
# COCREATE: CREATE WHAT MATTERS MOST

Do you feel like you're becoming a more in-control, chilled-out version of yourself?

In Part Three, you took charge of your life while continuing to apply your most useful tool, LTY. You carved out space to allow yourself to persevere through crises and challenges with gratitude. You learned to chill to redefine how accessible you want to be (and to whom). Then you looked inside to take a deeper dive into who you really are, and where you might be holding back. As you discovered what it meant to take control of your life, you allowed yourself to show up as the real you, at which point the sun—your spirit—started shining.

Now that you have gained more control over your business and life, you are ready to cocreate at a whole new level. The next three chapters empower you to construct the life you envision for yourself and with others, rather than simply making a plan that you may or may not execute. You must work for what you want, which no one can do for you. By doing so, you will get in tune with your emotions and rely on yourself more. Then you will shift your perspective to cherish your inner circle. Finally, you'll figure out that you can renew your energy when you stop overthinking and get going.

As you connect with yourself on a deeper level, you rely more on yourself and learn more about yourself in a way that will shape your life experience. This leads to co-creation (with your real self and with others) aligned with your wants and needs. As you enact changes to brighten your life, your potential accomplishments are endless. Let's begin with giving yourself permission to feel your emotions.

## CHAPTER 8
# FEEL YOUR EMOTIONS

Have you ever experienced a loss that left you feeling adrift?

I walked along Diamond Beach in Wildwood Crest, New Jersey, watching the sunrise. My meditative daily sunrise walks were usually a highlight of the week. The cool morning ocean breeze, water under my sandy toes, and sounds of seagulls typically washed away any stress in an instant. On that day, the ocean mist mixed with my salty tears stung my face.

Three days before leaving town for our annual Wildwood Crest family vacation, we said goodbye to Roxy, our eighteen-year-old, twelve-pound, brown-and-white Irish Jack Russell terrier.

I loved that little dog. And she was gone. *Is a part of me gone too?* It sure felt like it.

As I strolled along the beach, the morning sun touched my face as eighteen years of memories played in my mind. Being present was beyond challenging. My thoughts were more about the past and not about the wet sand between my toes. I was present enough to know I wasn't present.

*Why am I so distraught about this little dog?*

At that moment, I realized my emotional state wasn't just about Roxy. I had experienced the loss of close loved ones. However, the passing of Roxy had a different, complex effect on me. This wasn't just about a dog's passing. This was about almost two decades of life passing.

Given the situation, I kept walking, letting my mind wander where it wanted to go. I needed to feel these intense emotions before I could release them.

Although I grew up with dogs my entire life, Roxy was incredible. We had found each other. We had chosen each other. In the beginning, it was just her and me.

I replayed the moment she leaped into my lap in Jack Russell fashion on a sunny June morning. She had looked at me, pleading "make me yours," and I remembered that like it was yesterday. From the moment our eyes and hearts connected, she loyally navigated a huge chunk of life with me. Then with my husband, son, and me.

As I kept walking, memories flowed rapidly. Roxy had accompanied me through relationships, engagement, cancer, a new house, marriage, career moves, home renovations, a new baby, train rides, car rides, and more. I remembered the distressing day I found out I had thyroid cancer. She was there. And the day I came home from the hospital stay following my surgery to remove that cancer, she was there. I flashed back to the day we brought our son home from the NICU. She was there to delicately greet him with tender sniffs and licks. I recalled the night I dug inside my closet and myself. She had been there too. For all my lows and all my highs, she was there.

*No wonder I felt the way I did. She was with me through it all for eighteen years, without judgment, conflict, or criticism.*

Engulfed in serious thought, I had unknowingly traveled a few miles more than my normal route. I didn't mind. Time alone in the ocean air was helping me process raw emotions.

Back to the mental movie footage.

Roxy had an all-access pass to me. She knew everything a dog could learn about me from almost two decades of glances, scents, habits, and schedules. Every morning, we had kicked off the day with my early morning coffee. Roxy, me, and twelve ounces of hot, black coffee sat in silence.

Every night, she had nuzzled her little snout next to me. No matter how the day had transpired, I always felt content knowing she was right there with me.

In 2017, Roxy's health started to decline. The vet told me she was on "borrowed time." Roxy must have heard her because she healed herself, living a rejuvenated life for almost four more years.

Our family believed she was fueled by love. Her new diet of homemade beef, chicken, and vegetables didn't hurt. When I lost my job that same year, I had time and energy to care for her the way she had cared for me—absolutely, positively, unconditionally.

Life has a way of working out when we trust that it will.

Roxy continued to bounce back physically. After one set of miraculously improved blood labs yielding "normal" results, the vet said something like, "I don't even know what to say; she's remarkable." This memory made me smile through my heavy tears.

Roxy's resilience *was* remarkable. Roxy wanted to keep loving her life. She was inspiring.

In 2020, her zest for life continued while her little body slowed down. This was a bit ironic since the entire world had slowed down that same year. We were given bonus family time with her when she needed us most. Cataracts had taken her eyesight. She relied on sounds and smells. We learned to help her follow our voices. We used tapping methods to guide her to things like food. Roxy's memory guided her to her cozy bed and blankets, which were kept in the same spots they'd always been. We carried her up and down the stairs and into and out of the car.

I kept walking on that beach ... thinking, walking, and remembering.

Despite all this, she chose to stay with us. Some mornings, simply looking at her curled up in our bed inspired me to live a fuller life. She always seemed like she was exactly where she wanted to be. She felt like she belonged with us.

During Roxy's slow-down-and-seek-comfort phase, she was there for more milestones. The day I started my company, she was with me. She also became my little writing muse. She loved when I wrote or worked because it meant lap time and pets for her. One of the best perks of working from home was feeling her warmth.

*How am I ever going to feel that way again?*

Back to the mental movie footage.

Tuesday, August 17, 2021, felt like an extraordinary day. Roxy showed an abundant burst of boundless, happy energy that afternoon. She was interested in sunbathing and walking around much more than usual. In the late afternoon, we sat outside basking together in the sunshine. As I prepared dinner, she was more attached to me than ever. Roxy followed me around the kitchen, rubbing her face against my legs like a cat. At one point, she was climbing up my legs. She wanted to be in my arms. So I scooped her up.

That night, we relaxed on the sofa to watch the Yankees game on TV as a family. She was on my lap. In a split second, life changed. Suddenly, her earlier behavior on that memorable Tuesday made total sense. Roxy knew she was leaving.

Roxy's "borrowed" time ended within eighteen hours.

That scene I didn't want to keep seeing in my mind. I had already watched every minute of it with gut-wrenching sadness, and once was enough. I closed my blurry eyes, wiped away tears, and stopped the footage.

When I opened my eyes, I saw a much needed dose of dogs, walking with their owners, playing fetch, and jumping in the surf. That simple sight uplifted me too.

As I walked off the beach, I refocused on feeling grateful for our family's joyful time with Roxy. This remarkable dog taught our family valuable life skills that became part of our character. Part of us today. Part of us forever.

The next day, during my sunrise beach walk, I still felt sad, pensive, and messy. Our son longed for another dog. He was researching dog breeds and rescues with my husband. I totally understood. Meanwhile, I wasn't yet able to see through the fog of grief. I didn't feel ready to start a new life with a new dog. I didn't even feel like myself.

*Why did I feel so adrift between my past, present, and future?*

I had to pull it together for my family. I had a few more miles of walking time to regroup. Roxy was an integral part of my past. Now she was gone, and I had a lot more living to do.

After watching the sun rise and shine, I asked for a sign about what should come next. Then I headed back to the condo to try to start a better day. I was on family vacation after all.

The rest of the week went by fast and slow simultaneously. Friday morning, I woke up early again for my last sunrise beach walk of the week. I hadn't discovered any "signs" yet; I still felt periodically engulfed by emotional waves of grief.

As I moved my body forward, I wasn't sure how to move my life forward. My husband and son were encouraging me to go with them to "just look" at puppies. You know how that goes.

*What's next?*

Suddenly, the "sign" I longed for appeared. Two playful dogs charged past me to frolic in the ocean. One was a little white terrier type; the other was a large black retriever.

Sensing there was important meaning in this for me, I immediately stopped walking to observe the scene. These two adorable dogs and their owner were present together, enjoying their morning playtime.

I smiled, understanding Roxy's message from beyond—that one big *and* one small dog were heading our way. Furthermore, I would feel present, happy, and whole again.

*How are two different dogs going to find us?*

It didn't matter how. I walked off the beach that last balmy day of vacation feeling lighter under the calm, blue sky. I trusted that somehow, in some way, it was already unfolding. Although we weren't looking forward to going home to a dogless house, I felt more at peace.

## Reflect

Roxy's spirit was never lost. She was an inspirational master of resilience and determination. Even in the final hour, she showed her resolve.

She held on until my husband arrived to say goodbye, until we were a unified family. Then she closed her eyes to rest in peace with all four of us together.

Once her tiny body was gone, my spirit felt lost. During sunrise walks along Diamond Beach in August 2021, my legs moved forward. Time moved forward. *I* could *not* move forward. When the "sign" I longed for appeared, the simplistic, two-word lesson landed via two playful dogs bolting past me to splash in the water.

**Trust yourself.**

This was an intense, unpleasant period in my forty-something life. The more I tried to push or pull myself through the emotional muck, the more stressed and adrift I felt.

The day I asked for a sign, I listened to myself. I was admitting I needed to move on. I also realized I must remain open to new possibilities. The idea of new beginnings arrived in the form of a big and little dog along my sandy sunrise walk path.

The message wrapped in that cute dog scene was that I needed to trust myself. Trust that the emotional rip current would pass. Trust that I would ride the waves, making the right decision for my family. Trust that I could navigate *any* situation.

I had to trust myself.

Why did I choose to share this experience? Because even if you've never had a dog, you can relate to the experience of loss. Grief is real, whether it's for a dog, a human, a job, a business, a home, or anything else that impacts your life. At some point, we all navigate the impact of loss.

Loss reminds you that chunks of your life are now mere memories. Loss reminds you that moments really do matter. Loss reminds you that you are still alive. Loss reminds you to trust yourself to find your way forward.

> **Loss doesn't have to mean you have to lose yourself.**

As a result of living eighteen years with Roxy, I gained unconditional love, trust, and companionship from a dog who knew me to my core. Loss doesn't have to mean you have to lose yourself. After her passing, I gained the ability to trust myself. This lesson comes everywhere with me. It serves to complement LTY.

If you LTY, you know when you feel off-kilter. When you trust yourself, you know when to ask for guidance, be open to receiving it, and use it to be an active participant in your life. If I had let my sad mental state shut my openness during that last sunrise walk in August 2021, I would have missed the sign of two dogs encouraging me to find fulfillment again.

During the rough days that accompany a heartbreaking loss, you aren't looking for immediate solutions—although you will want them at times. You are simply trying to walk forward, repositioning yourself in your life without whatever or whoever you lost.

Although this lesson came to me through a difficult loss, it's about more than loss. When you process your emotions, allow yourself to get messy, and then pull yourself together, you enable yourself to remain open to living your best life. You become ready to receive the guidance you need when you need it. You own the ability to listen to yourself, ask for guidance, and receive guidance, rather than allowing it to get buried by grief, resistance, and doubt.

If you build trust with yourself, you can guide yourself through daunting times. If you don't trust yourself, crashing waves can keep you down. How can you enjoy the sunrise when you're toppled by waves?

And the waves of life ebb and flow. Fast-forward one year later to Summer 2022. We traveled to the same family vacation spot. On the first day of vacation, I rose early for my sunrise walk along Diamond Beach.

This time, I felt joyful, appreciative, and free. Over the past year, joy had replaced sorrow. Smiles replaced those salty tears. Momentum replaced inaction.

Two dogs found us. Although we explored dog rescues as an option, that didn't work out this time. Remember the dog my son and husband wanted to go "see?" Well, we went to Cream Puff Labradoodles in New Jersey to "just look" at "blue band boy." The minute my husband and I watched the puppy sprint to greet our son, we knew that was that. His old soul, gentle eyes, happy wagging tail, and the white fluffy star-shaped marking on his chest told us he was the one. Rockie, a cuddly, handsome, apricot Australian labradoodle came home with us that same sunny September 2021 afternoon.

Before Thanksgiving 2021, Penny joined our family from Connemara Terriers in Maine. Penny is a smooth-coat, white-and-brown, Irish Jack Russell terrier. Roxy was also a smooth-coat, white-and-brown, Irish Jack Russell Terrier. Penny was born in August, two days before Roxy passed away. Penny and Roxy are *a lot* alike.

We turned the page as a connected family to write a new chapter together.

We can trust our own guidance to navigate the unknown. Let's practice how to feel emotions to ride life's roughest waves.

## Learn

We all experience loss at some point in our lives. When navigating loss, it can feel nearly impossible to stay present. You know that only you have the power to pull yourself together. The problem is you feel like you don't have the will; you don't know what to do next because you long for what you lost.

As a result, you face even more pressure than usual. You try to sort through an array of emotions, hold yourself together, and lead your career. You get frustrated because you want to be able to surf the seas like a professional.

Meanwhile, you are treading in deep water, thinking so much that you forget how to swim. It might sound something like this:

> *I feel like part of me is gone.*
> *I don't know what to do next.*

*I don't know how I'm "supposed" to feel.*
*Others expect me to just move on.*
*No one knows what I'm going through.*
*No one feels the way I do. I want to feel "myself" again.*

While you're trying to keep your head above water, a lack of awareness or care from others creates more emotional waves. It's possible they don't know how you feel, or they pass verbal judgment about how you feel. For example, after Roxy's death, someone looked at me dismissively and said, "You only lost a dog." Did the person own a dog? Any pet? A goldfish, even? No, no, and no. Other common expressions that can cause waves include the phrases "at least" or "move on."

Such commentary only adds to your angst. None of it helps you.

So you retreat to your mental footage. You get yourself in a cycle of replaying uplifting past memories because they comfort you. When the footage stops, you realize that no memory, no matter how good, will bring back who or what you lost.

Then you feel sad. You feel emptier. You aren't helping yourself, but you are too consumed by your grief to realize it. That's okay.

Of course, you *want* to move on. You know it's on you to figure it out.

*Trust yourself.*

The only time you can move on is when you're ready. The only way you can get through your emotional hurricane is by helping yourself.

What does it look like to help yourself?

As we covered in the last chapter, looking inside yourself can help you show up as the real you. Here, we are learning how trusting yourself can help you steer all aspects of your life.

When you run a business, you're often expected (by yourself and others) to have everything figured out. How do you figure out how to bounce back from something that jolted you to your core? How do you lead your business when you're preoccupied watching old movies in your mind?

You're supposed to know what to do.

Well, you must focus on what matters most. What matters most in the now is the life in front of you. Not the parts of life in your rearview mirror. When you come to grips with this reality, you are ready to move on. Not because someone told you to. Because *you* are ready.

You are ready to get back to living. You are ready to be present and engage with those around you. You are ready to deliver first-rate customer experience. You are ready to feel your own happiness again.

How do you begin? Get out your most valuable tool. LTY. You will never lose it. So use it.

As I've said before, LTY will help you persevere through the most trying times. LTY more closely to build trust with yourself. Focus on trusting your intuition.

## Apply

When a wave crashes down, washing away someone or something in your life, it can pull you underwater for a while. During these rough periods, you can apply LTY to sense when you need to connect with your inner guidance system. At this point, you know LTY will help you focus on allowing yourself to feel your emotions (and salty tears), accept what is (a loss), and build trust with yourself (first).

> **Be your flashlight.**

The process of building trust with yourself transpires in the space between what you truly know about yourself and what you *think* you know about yourself. Ironically, this is the space where you have gotten a little (or a lot) stuck or lost because you doubt that you have the strength, resilience, or stamina to pull yourself up. However, you do. You can use your inner navigation system to trust yourself and gain clarity by following these three steps:

1. **LTY. Acknowledge what you know about yourself—both the positives and the challenges.** You don't need analytics, numbers, or logic. Yes, I said that. Instead, you need faith in yourself, wonder about yourself, and the desire to truly know yourself. Do you think you are too stuck to move on? Do you think you don't have as much resilience as you do? Do you think you are worn down or weak? Whatever the case, you need to shift from what you think you know about yourself to what you actually know about yourself.

    Then accept it. Acknowledge that you lived through whatever rough situation you faced. Acknowledge that you founded a business. Acknowledge that you lead your own career. Acknowledge that you are loved. Your list of personal experiences goes on. The point is to recognize yourself as a whole person, with knowledge, behaviors, and emotions, who can loosen their grip on limiting beliefs.

    This shift is necessary to start trusting yourself. Trust that you won't be adrift for long. Trust that you are strong, resilient, and determined. Trust that you are ready to make independent choices. You don't need to rely on others to tell you what you can figure out about yourself.

2. **Turn on your intuitive power.** Now that you have acknowledged more of the truth about yourself, you can activate your intuition. I'll pause here to say I'm not guiding you toward magical thinking or superstitious beliefs. Furthermore, I do not recommend you make business decisions involving money, risk, and regulations based on "gut feel." I am guiding you toward using the intuitive power you already hold to help you trust yourself. You don't need to be buried in data to trust yourself. You hold all the research findings you need because you have lived your life.

    Just as you can access LTY at any time, you can also access your intuitive power at any time. These tools do not disappear when you encounter unfortunate circumstances. When you feel adrift, part of the reason is that your emotions, like grief, have caused you to lose your tools. You haven't lost yourself. Even in the dark, you can find your tools again when you trust yourself to be the light you need.

*How?*
By trusting that you will guide yourself.
*Even in the dark?*
Yes. Be your flashlight.
*What is the biggest obstacle?*
Thinking that you can't.
*What is another big obstacle?*
Looking externally for facts that aren't always available or relevant.
*Why am I so quick to assume I can't do, or be, this or that?*
Because we can condition ourselves to think we can't do, or be, more.

Overcoming thoughts and behaviors ingrained in yourself is a process that requires commitment and patience. It starts with realizing answers are not always embedded in facts, reasoning, and analytics. Sometimes, the only person you need to reason with is yourself. Ask me how I know.

You can build trust in yourself. This means that you remain calm, stay courageous, and use your wisdom to address your personal and business challenges.

3. **Find your own answers.** When you seek answers to your unique needs and problems, there is no instant gratification. As you build trust in yourself, you will loosen your grip, release doubt, and find solutions.

    You don't have all the answers. No one does. You can find more than you thought you could. Let's walk through how building trust can lead you to find answers.

    One day, you find yourself faced with an inevitable loss. As you muddle through your daily life, you feel sad, confused, and stuck. There is no-one-size-fits-all textbook emotional response to a loss. You feel your way.

    When you trust yourself, you can influence your outcomes. For example, you realize that you can LTY. So you dig deeper into your feelings. Then you can tap into your intuitive powers to ask for guidance. This can be done by focusing on a statement that makes sense to you, such as, "Show me the way forward." By asking for guidance, you are admitting you don't have the answers. You are asking yourself (and if your belief system goes there, a higher power) for help.

Next, you allow yourself to be open to receiving the answer, guidance, sign, or whatever you want to call it. This requires relinquishing control, which may seem a bit counterintuitive since Part Three focused on the importance of control. The point here is that even as a business owner, you don't need to control *everything*. You control you. You don't control everyone and everything else because that's not how co-creation works.

While finding your answers, patience is required. Based on my experience, business owners aren't the most patient types. Practice patience as you build trust in yourself. Patience is your best friend.

As you discover your solutions, recognize the wisdom you possess, as well as the wisdom you need to make the best decisions for you and your business. When there is a knowledge gap, admit it. Then seek the help you need to fill in the gap you identified.

As you practice trusting yourself, you will develop a rhythm of asking for and receiving guidance. If you remain open to receiving guidance, you can find your way forward with increased confidence in your reliable inner guidance system.

When you trust yourself, you gain tremendous clarity. Although we explored this lesson through the lens of a business owner experiencing loss and the subsequent tumultuous period that follows, trusting yourself comes in handy in other situations.

For example, when you truly LTY, your intuition will tell you whether someone is the right individual to earn your trust. If something feels off with someone, it likely is. LTY. Think about a time you were in a relationship where something felt off. You ignored your feelings because you believed what the other person said to you or did in front of you. You relied on those situational "facts."

Now let's look at a relatable business example: hiring a new employee. You were attracted to the person's resume, so you scheduled an interview. During the interview, they said what you wanted to hear. However, you felt like something wasn't quite right. Since you desperately needed help, you hired them anyway. Why? Because you relied on the "facts" on paper married with what they said to your face. Maybe you told yourself you're too picky or you could train the person for the job. Well, fast-forward. The person turned out to be a bad fit for you, your team, and the company. The hire was a managerial nightmare not truly qualified to perform at the level they presented themselves. They were 100 percent *not* moldable.

The consequence of not listening to your intuition? Headaches, stress, and more work. Plus, you lost time you will never get back. In this situation, your initial instinct was your intuition. You dismissed it. In the end, you were right. The damage was already done. In a way, you dismissed yourself. Why? Because you didn't trust yourself.

As you become comfortable trusting yourself more and more, you can extend your practice to build trust with others. There are good reasons why companies utilize team-building retreats and trust exercises as group development tools. When you trust yourself and others, you can elevate the group's potential as a whole. Think about it in the context of business and personal relationships. Building trust can benefit business outcomes, including client acquisition, customer retention, and team environment. With respect to personal relationships, building trust solidifies mutually beneficial exchanges within your inner circle, fostering co-creation. The inner circle is a concept we will explore in the next chapter.

Leading your professional and personal lives goes more smoothly when you trust yourself. This is because you become more willing to explore the unknown. You seek realistic answers to your needs and problems. You don't fear the next wave that will crash down because you trust yourself to make the right choices to mold your own life in *any* situation.

Let's practice building, the kind that taps into your curiosity, creativity, and confidence.

## Act: The Sandcastle

To help you trust yourself and your inner guidance to create a new phase in your life, this exercise will reconnect you with the natural trust in yourself you had as a child whenever you created something new. For this exercise, you are going to tap into your creativity to build an *imaginary* sandcastle.

Imaginary? Yes, I know you are a professional adult. Trust me; flow with it.

Imagine yourself as a child visiting the beach, seeing the expanse of sand and waves before you. All you can think about is building a sandcastle. This sandcastle is envisioned by you. Built by you. Molded by you with your bare hands.

No two sandcastles are the same. There are different formations, heights, widths. Elaborate works of sandcastle art can enter the realm of sculpture. Similar to building a business, when building a sandcastle, there is no limit to your vision.

For the purposes of this imaginary project, you aren't using your left brain. Don't research what beaches have the best sand, calculate the perfect sand-to-water ratio, or use fancy tools.

This is an exercise in using your creative mind. You are building this sandcastle yourself without co-creation or collaboration because this is an exercise in trusting yourself.

Here's what you need:

- **Tool:** LTY. You are listening to yourself about what, when, where, and how to build what you want to construct. Let your imaginary hands go where your mind takes you.

Also, you're not asking someone for advice, input, or approval. You're working independently while trusting yourself.
- **Materials:** Your imagination plus imaginary water and sand are all you need.

    Envision your sandcastle in your mind's eye and use your imagination to build it now.

    As you "work" with nature, keep in mind that you can't force it. If your proportion of water and sand aren't quite right, you won't be able to create the intended structure, no matter how hard you try. Too much water, the sand won't mold. With too little water, the formation will crumble.

    At this point, you may be wondering, *Why am I doing this? What is really going on here?* You trust that you can use what you've got to build what you set out to build. You are tapping into your creativity, independence, and will to succeed. Think of the sandcastle as a phase of life you are envisioning and building for yourself.
- **Attitude:** Patience is the most useful attitude here. It's okay if you don't get the right mix the first time. Make an adjustment, try again, and you'll get it.

    You know from making sandcastles as a kid or with your family members that you can't rush it. It takes time and patience. Think slow and steady.

Admire the beautiful sandcastle molded with your own hands, imagination, and patience in your mind. You created it.

No matter how many barriers you craft to protect your castle, a wave will come and wash it away. Don't spend time building barriers. Instead, revel in the fact that you created something beautiful on your own. Most importantly, now you trust yourself to know what to do to rebuild it.

Now that you've reconnected with the trust and creativity you've always had within you, what phase of your life will you build next?

*Remember, trusting yourself enables you to build and rebuild any aspect of your life.*

## Ask

1. Have you ever experienced a loss that resulted in you feeling stuck? How did you get unstuck?
2. Before you read this chapter, did you trust yourself to seek and receive guidance when you needed it? What insight or action will you put into practice to help you trust yourself?

## SOLIDIFY WHAT YOU'VE LEARNED

◊ **LESSON 1:** Change course when a new path feels right.

◊ **LESSON 2:** Collect skills and confidence.

◊ **LESSON 3:** Let the strength of kindness flow through you.

◊ **LESSON 4:** Stay driven in the moment to excel under pressure.

◊ **LESSON 5:** Persevere with gratitude.

◊ **LESSON 6:** Redefine what accessibility means to you.

◊ **LESSON 7:** Choose to show up as the real you.

◊ **LESSON 8:** Trust yourself.

## CHAPTER 9
# SHIFT YOUR PERSPECTIVE

Have you ever discovered deeper meaning in something you treasured?

It was a typical busy morning. As I stood in front of my mirror, blow-drying my hair, a glint of light on the bathroom counter caught my eye. Following my Grandma Ann's passing more than twenty years earlier, my mom had given me this pocket-sized keepsake. One side is a mirror, the other a picture of Grandma Ann, her mother.

Instantly, I was transported back to that Sunday spring morning when I returned to my dorm after breakfast and received a phone message from my father, asking me to call back when I could.

My usual routine was to call my parents on Sunday evenings. What couldn't wait until tonight?

When I called back, my father answered the phone after not even a full ring. His voice quivered, which was out of character for my calm and steady dad. I knew this wasn't going to be good. He gently informed me that my Grandma Ann had passed away suddenly during the night.

The air got sucked out of the room. Speechless, I gripped my desk as I sat down slowly in my chair. I couldn't talk or cry or move. At that moment, I could only be still.

Palm Sunday would never be the same. Neither would Easter.

By Tuesday night, I was home from college to spend a few days with my family and push through the services. Craving comfort within the finality of the loss, I kept replaying my most recent memory with my grandma.

I recalled the prior weekend. I had come home from Villanova for an unplanned visit. During that time, I enjoyed some impromptu quality time with Grandma Ann. We talked, laughed, and watched TV. Of course, we shared a tasty meal because one of her love languages was homemade food cooked with care.

Something had compelled me to come home that weekend. At nineteen, I had listened to myself, without realizing it. Now I was beyond grateful that I did. When I closed my eyes, I could *feel* her presence from that most recent day.

For my entire life, Grandma Ann had been a peaceful presence of unconditional love and support. I adored her. She was an integral part of my family's warmth and stability. And now she was gone.

Relentless questions flooded my mind. *Why now? Why so suddenly? Why? She wasn't even sick.*

I knew there were no answers. Seeking a spot to lay my heavy head on a pillow, I retreated to my bedroom. Lying on my pink comforter and fluffy pillow, I closed my eyes.

Then I smiled, remembering the way she toasted and buttered an English muffin to absolute perfection, with literally every nook and cranny having the perfect amount of warm, melted butter; the way she sat on her gold, velvety sofa wearing her favorite pink wool cardigan, while lightly combing my little-girl long brown hair in the most tranquil way; and the way she and her sweet, petite sister made the most delicious lemon ice and decadent Italian ricotta cookies from scratch.

I remembered the way she taught me to cook and bake, to play solitaire and build with Lincoln Logs on her comfortable living room carpet, and to thread a needle and sew a button.

I remembered the way we played hide-and-seek for hours; the way she walked me home from elementary school; and the way she let me stay up late to watch "grown-up" television shows with her.

Fond memories kept pouring in, like the way she used to make me fresh, hot coffee with lots of creamy milk; the way she used to let me sip red wine out of my own "adult" glass at family Sunday dinners; and the way her smooth, beautiful porcelain skin maintained its youthful firmness into her seventies.

And the loving way she raised her daughter to eventually become my special, nurturing mother (also with spectacular skin).

As the memories flowed, I remembered the sincere way we immensely loved each other. Every nook and cranny of her, and my mother, was filled with love.

Following the love-filled thoughts that brought tears and smiles, an odd feeling of numbness set in. This was somewhat helpful because the next thing I knew, I was wearing a depressing, suffocating black suit while standing in front of a church altar adorned with fresh funeral flowers.

I rose to the occasion and adored my Grandma Ann, as she had adored me for my whole life. As I read the blurry words in front of me, I couldn't hear my voice or see what was going on around me. Except I did notice the sadness pouring out of my mom, who had just lost her last surviving parent.

After the vivid memories faded, I transported myself back to the present moment.

Currently, I was a business owner, wife, mom, and daughter trying to make sense of it all. "It" being my life experience. I casually glanced back down at the keepsake on my vanity that had sent me back in time.

This treasure, more than eighty years old, "lives" on my vanity as an inspiration. Every morning, I smile at it. Every night, I think of Gram.

Grandma Ann and I shared an immeasurable bond. She had an angelic, calming presence. We talked about anything and everything without judgment. She was like a beacon of light, filled with gentle guidance when I needed it. She often said to me, "What is meant to be will be." That was her gentle reminder to let life unfold in due time.

During some chapters of my life, those words, in her soothing voice, echoed in my mind, reminding me to keep the faith. Entrepreneurship certainly is a test in the "faith" department.

As the blow-dryer hummed, so did my mind. I had owned this two-sided token for more than two decades. However, on this particular day, I comprehended a meaningful message wrapped in symbolism.

On one side was a black-and-white image of a young, twenty-eight-year-old brunette woman with a soft smile, dressed as a bridesmaid, taken the day of her sister's wedding. The image is of the woman who became my beloved grandma.

Despite the thousands of times I had glanced at this photo, this time I observed something different. I didn't just see a woman dressed up for a celebratory occasion. I *felt* the warmth, love, and happiness bundled into her true presence. I cherished her then. I cherish her now.

On the other side was a mirror. I held up the little mirror and looked into it. Grandma Ann played an early role in contributing to the life experience of the now-grown woman reflected back at me in that mirror.

For decades, the face in that mirror was Grandma Ann's. Now it was mine. And I could see Gram's presence reflected there as well.

## **Reflect**

Why was I intent on exploring this little treasure now?

I was seeking deeper meaning. I was ready to learn more about myself in a way that could shape my life experiences.

I turned off the hairdryer, finished getting dressed, and opened my dresser drawer. I took out the only article of my grandma's clothing I had saved all these years: her pink cardigan sweater. I gathered pen and paper. Then I sat down with the mirror and her comfy sweater.

I felt one of those memorable "wow" discoveries brewing, like a fresh pot of coffee that smells so good, you can taste it before you even pour it. Although I was excited about the freshness of it all, I reminded myself to be patient.

As I held Grandma Ann's dear pink sweater, Rockie and Penny inspected it with their noses. Their bright, inquisitive eyes glanced at me, sensing my pensiveness.

After her passing, Gram and I had stayed connected through memories, "signs," and even some divine dreams. One of our signs includes "pennies from heaven." She collected pennies found along her path after my grandfather passed away. Now, my mom and I collect the ones we notice.

Today, I didn't need any shiny pennies. The sign appeared in the form of a lesson along with my reflection in her small keepsake mirror.

**Cherish your inner circle.**

When Grandma Ann closed her compassionate, brown eyes to rest in peace, her angelic spirit and love kept living. I saw it in myself when I looked into the mirror. Our formative bond was so strong that all these years later, I easily recall the scent of her sweet, iconic Chanel N°5 perfume, hear her soft, soothing voice, and feel our enduring mutual adoration.

So why did I choose to share this story? Because having someone in your life who helped shape who, what, and how you see yourself in the mirror today is priceless. Perhaps parts of *who* you see in the mirror can be attributed to the unconditional love and support you received during your formative years. Or the rough stuff you survived. Perhaps you learned to be more appreciative of *what* you see in the mirror. *How* you see yourself may have been influenced by the uncommon folks in your life who accepted you for the real you.

When you recognize who is in your inner circle, you can express gratitude for the unconditional love, trust, and companionship they provide. You *feel* it.

Grandma Ann was one of those uncommon humans in my life. For nineteen years, she was a foundational, positive part of my upbringing. Since she wasn't a parent or a friend, she helped me see myself differently. I felt her everlasting love every day—even when we weren't together, like when I went off to college.

Although I didn't realize it then, I know now that she will always be a constant part of my genuine, loyal inner circle. Her support didn't end when she physically left my world. Her unconditional love will never fade because it's ingrained in me.

After all these years, I was connecting dots about the value of certain relationships. I scribbled down a few more ideas with both dogs by my side.

Within the past couple of years, I've learned to surround myself with like-minded, genuine friends and family (and dogs) for two reasons. First, reciprocal relationships *feel* good. Second, *our inner circle matters*. It matters because we truly support each other through highs, lows, and everything in between. We respect each other. Plus, we want each other to succeed. There is no judgment, deceit, or drama. We give because we want to, not to get something in return. As a result, we feel lifted, respected, and valued. That is worth cherishing.

Then something else clicked. My life experience was shifting because my perspective had shifted. As my lens narrowed to focus on my inner circle, my view of life widened to include a bigger picture of what mattered most. I fully recognized that I had the strength to navigate my own career and personal life with those I *wanted* to be part of my experiences. My inner circle could be part of my journey. In turn, I could be part of theirs.

At this point in my life, this lesson comes everywhere with me. I've realized that my inner circle affects more than my personal life. My positive experiences with the ones I adore allow me to feel energized, peaceful, and appreciative—all of which serve as fuel for enhanced professional performance.

Members of your inner circle may pass away or fade away as your lives evolve. However, the way they impact your life experience lives forever. More importantly, cherishing the most special friends and family in your life while they are with you helps you all enjoy the present.

Of course, you don't have to experience the loss of someone in your inner circle to understand this lesson. You can cherish your most treasured past and present relationships as your inner circle right now.

Once you shift your perspective, you understand that support from close confidants helps you live your life differently, in a good way. Let's explore how you can nurture yourself and your inner circle to appreciate your reflection in the mirror.

## Learn

At some point in your life, you learn that the quality of your relationships directly correlates with your quality of life. When you hit highs and lows in your life, you can see who lifts you up, who rises to meet you, and who wanders away. That's when you understand that real relationships are far more important than your number of "friends." You realize the value of a trusted inner circle.

What exactly is an inner circle?

An inner circle consists of a few supportive, genuine, and open-minded friends or family members who help you see yourselves differently, entirely, and more positively.

Why is this important? Well, everyone needs to regularly renew themselves. When you run a business, access to reliable outlets helps you recharge. Having a trustworthy inner circle becomes a valuable asset in this regard.

If you're like most business owners, the problem is you have so much going on in your own life that it's hard to cultivate your inner circle, let alone cherish it. Therefore, you face some of your impediments head-on, with less emotional support because in your mind, it's easier that way. On the career front, you may not share your celebrations often because you believe others won't care or you don't have extra time. You get frustrated because you *want* to share more of your life's happenings with a few others. To some extent, you even feel like you *need to* because you're getting bottled up inside.

However, you're not sure who is in your inner circle—and you don't have the energy to figure it out. Your internal dialogue may sound like this:

*I don't have time to be social.*
*I don't know who I can trust.*
*I'll keep it to myself.*
*I want trustworthy advice.*
*I need someone else to talk to about this.*
*I feel like they don't really care.*
*I feel like I don't have "real" friends.*
*I'm so done with drama, gossip, and criticism.*

While you're trying to identify your true supporters, you may encounter some eye-opening experiences. For example, someone whom you thought was inner-circle caliber took you by unpleasant surprise at a social event by asking you too-personal questions. You learned the hard way that another is way too competitive, dramatic, and selfish. Someone mistakenly thought that inner circle means inner knowledge about your finances. None of these types belong in your inner circle. Move on.

After such experiences, you may think you don't have bandwidth for this nonsense. In a way, you're right. That's okay. However, you do need to make time for the ones who *belong* in your inner circle.

As we covered in the last chapter, feeling your emotions can help you trust yourself. Here, we are learning the importance of shifting your perspective to recognize who is in your inner circle and cherish the ones who love and support the real you.

So how do you recognize who is in *your* inner circle? When you're with them, you notice positive effects.

*It's easier to chill and be yourself.* There's no effort made to act or look a certain way. You can be the real you without judgment or criticism. You enjoy being in their company. A sense of calm flows from a natural, more relaxed state of being.

*You look better.* After some quality inner-circle time, you may look in the mirror and notice you look happier, brighter, and more uplifted. Meanwhile, the only treatment or injection you got was a dose of uninterrupted, in-person conversation with a special someone who makes you feel upbeat.

*You feel better.* As you begin to recognize that your inner circle matters, in part because reciprocal relationships *feel* fantastic, you may also notice that you're more accepting of the reflection you see in the mirror.

Inner-circle relationships are reciprocal relationships filled with unquestioned love, support, and acceptance. And when you receive all those benefits from your inner circle, you'll want to cherish them in return.

## Apply

Your vigorous life stirs up a lot of emotions from day to day, week to week, month to month, year to year. Some days, when you look in the mirror, you may see yourself as happy, relaxed, and peaceful. Other times, you may see a stressed, uneasy, and tired face staring back at you. LTY will lead you to sense when you crave some feel-good vibes around you.

> **Your most valuable relationships grow hardy through conscious caring.**

Sharing simple, enjoyable moments with your inner circle has the unique ability to brighten your day and your face. Think of it as part of your emotional wellness. Although your inner circle will primarily include your personal relationships, these relationships will pay dividends in all areas of your life.

Let the cherishing begin by following these three steps:

1. **Cherish yourself.** To cultivate your inner circle, start with appreciating yourself. Build on what you learned in the last chapter about trusting yourself; trust that you are strong, resilient, and determined. And keep shifting.

    When you reach the cocreate phase, you see things from new perspectives. Your focus is different because you are different. This is a normal part of your evolution that comes with the life experience of good, bad, and everything in between. It's time to appreciate your complete self. You're more than a business owner, significant other, parent, child, sibling, or friend. Revel in that.

    Look in the mirror. Appreciate the real, beautiful you reflected back at you. You don't want to be looking toward your inner circle to give you the love and sense of self-worth you can only give yourself—that leads to codependency, neediness, and a need to receive that never ends. Cherishing yourself will give you the resources required to cherish your inner circle.

2. **Identify who is in your inner circle.** Before you can cherish your inner circle, you need to know who's in it. Examine your past and present relationships to identify your current, solid, close ones. Who loves and supports the real you?

    Although supervisors or colleagues can be huge supporters, I don't recommend including work relationships in your inner circle because you need to feel free to be the real you, without worrying about how it will impact your professional life. Here you're thinking about your closest friend whom you vented to *about* the supervisor. See the difference?

Now get inquisitive about the personal relationships you identified as current, solid, and close.

- Who has influenced you positively?
- What did you learn from them?
- How did they impact the person you are today?

As you contemplate your answers to these questions, you'll observe that some folks who influenced your development in the past are no longer in your orbit today. Your inner circle shifts as you shift. For example, you may you may have lost touch with your "best" friends in high school or college because your life moved on without them. Your inner circle can also shift if you move from one location to another or after you change relationships, marry, or become a parent. Your inner circle does not have to be static. After all, you're not.

So how about the inner-circle-caliber individuals in your life who have passed away? You can still consider them part of your inner circle of influence. They helped shape parts of who you are today, and their influence can continue to shape you. For example, recall my earlier story about Grandma Ann. Her passing didn't mean she exited my being. She lives within me. Your loved ones who depart this life can stay with you too.

Enough with the past examination. Now focus on your present situation. LTY while exploring some questions to help curate your inner circle.

- Who do you trust to lift you up or give you objective advice?
- Who do you feel loves you unconditionally?
- Who tells you the truth even when it's hard?
- What similarities do you share with the ones closest to you?
- Which of your relationships are reciprocal in nature?

Your answers will reveal the handful of trusted, uncommon individuals in your life who help you see yourself in new, more authentic ways. These are the individuals you can trust to be there for you. This is your sturdy foundation. This is your inner circle.

Less is more when it comes to the number of members in your inner circle. You don't need quantity. You don't need "followers." You don't need to be chasing status. If a so-called friend tries to isolate you or deflect attention away from your successes, that person is not suitable for your inner circle. If a relationship lacks trust, it's weak; if it's one-sided, you're doing too much work. You get the idea.

3. **Cherish your inner circle.** Now that you've identified your inner circle, recognize that these relationships require nurturing to endure through time. Think about it this way. You don't stay strong and healthy by being sedentary and eating junk food. You don't build muscle by staring at weights. You must lift them. Relationships require a lift too.

Your most valuable relationships grow hardy through conscious caring.

At this point, you are ready to cherish the most important folks in your life.

So what is stopping you? See if this sounds familiar.

*I feel like I'm running at an over-scheduled, frantic pace. I feel so tired at the end of my workday; I'd rather curl up to watch TV, read, or sleep than socialize. I feel too stressed to be good company for anyone.*

Okay, be real. What else is stopping you?

*I've been seeking external validation from others who will never reach inner-circle status. I've been sprinkling my energy around too much. The truth is I'm giving far more than I'm getting from certain relationships.*

Who cares what they think about you or your life? None of that matters. You can trust yourself, cherish yourself, and cultivate your inner circle.

LTY. When you stop focusing on things like trying to obtain some sort of validation or grow relationships that will never be more than "surface" relationships, you will free up resources to pay attention to those in your life who contribute to it rather than take from it.

Now what is stopping you?

*Nothing.*

So cherish the experience of traveling through life with special "someones" who energize you rather than drain you. Your happiness affects everyone and everything around you, including your significant others, dependents, and business relationships. It's worth investing in your own happiness.

Let's stay here to talk business for a bit. Your inner circle most likely consists of a handful of friends and family. Although your most valuable, core relationships do not need to include business colleagues from your company or your clients' companies, your inner-circle relationships directly affect your work world.

How?

Walk through this hypothetical scenario. You encountered a tough day at work because one of your prominent clients decided to put the next project out to bid. You now feel compelled to jump through some hoops to prove, again, that you are the right service provider to solve their problem. The whole thing is another "to do" on top of your never-ending, growing list of action items.

On top of this, the performance of one of your part-time associates has tanked. You need to have another discussion sooner rather than later. You sense that it won't go too well because this person doesn't get it. Then you start asking yourself why you even hired the help. Oh, how could you forget? You were desperate for a few more hours a week with your family. Now, here you are doing their work plus your work.

What do you do?

You LTY. You sense that you are ready to implode. So you vent to one of your best friends, whom you adore for their encouraging yet frank advice. She assures you that you can keep the business by continuing to do what you love while being the real you. As for the associate who is giving you a major headache, she reminds you that *you* run *your* company. She tells you sternly, "Act like it." Then she vents to you about her teenager who is testing her limits along with her patience. You remind her to use her best persuasion skills.

Even during this serious conversation, you laugh a lot about various things. In fact, laughter flows whenever you spend time together.

As a result, you each go back to your respective situations feeling refreshed, ready to do what you need to do. You win your client's next competitive bid project. You also decide to replace your underperforming associate. Your family notices you seem less stressed. And your friend uses your advice to improve her relationship with her teenager.

Do you see how the inner-circle friend positively impacted the business situation? You don't need colleagues from your business in your inner circle to help you with your business. In fact, you helped each other. You both aired, listened, and advised. You gave each other a boost, complete with a laughing fit.

These are the special individuals you want by your side as you travel through the bumps, twists, turns, zigzags, hills, and mountains of life. Cherishing them is simple.

*LTY.* Sense when you desire a dose of inner-circle time. Then make it happen.

*Show* them you care about them. Invite them to do something, buy a token gift for the holidays or their birthday, or anything that shows how you feel.

*Tell* them why you appreciate them. "I'm glad we spent time together yesterday—I woke up feeling so energized this morning."

*Share* a quick hello, even if it's a quick text message. "I was thinking about you today because . . ."

*Keep* them in your heart and mind even when you aren't physically together. Remember things that make you smile.

Enjoy their company now while you have the gift of time.

Your inner circle is a powerful asset with multiple benefits. It helps your professional and personal worlds feel easier. It helps the heavy life stuff feel lighter. Plus, when you look in the mirror, you see an enhanced version of yourself. You know you are cocreating with whom you want to exchange real and meaningful life experiences. You all want to cocreate candid conversations, belly-aching laughter, and personal memories to make your lives feel well lived. This is what matters.

Let's practice cherishing your solid inner circle with Cherish Rings.

## Act: Cherish Rings

To help you appreciate the relationships that truly matter, in this wellness exercise you will focus on the qualities of individuals you consider part of your inner circle.

In five steps, you're going to examine, visualize, and treasure each individual in your inner circle with Cherish Rings:

1. **Imagine a ring** representing each friend or family member in your inner circle. (If you prefer to draw these rings with paper and pen, then do so, although it's not necessary.)

    Feel free to include a circle for your pets; after all, you comfort, love, and support each other.

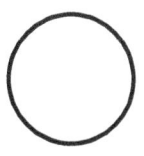

    ○

2. **Then, starting with the first individual, visualize words inside the ring that describe why you believe this person is exceptional.** Assemble a list of their attributes in your mind. For example, the first person who pops into your mind may stir up words like compassionate, accepting, trustworthy, honest, kind, generous, thoughtful, patient, sweet, and soothing. You may recall little things they do for you or that you do together, like helping you cook, baking the best homemade cookies, or traveling with you to explore new

destinations. They may have done something big for you, such as comforting you during a horrible loss or illness.

3. **Move on to the next individual, visualizing words that describe that person in a separate ring, until you have a ring for each member of your inner circle.** For example, the next person could be loving, accepting, trustworthy, honest, kind, funny, organized, disciplined, and so on. You may recall how much you laugh when you're together, how you exchange stories about all your dog's funny antics, and how you help each other navigate the phases of parenthood. You get the idea.

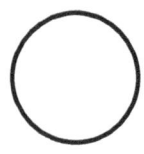

◯

After you go through this part of the exercise, you may have a handful or so of circles created. Even if you have just one or two circles filled with reasons why someone is treasured by you, you are blessed. There are no right or wrong answers, and no number is too few. As mentioned earlier, your inner circle is about quality, not quantity.

4. **Now pause.** Soak in all the positive thoughts you released into your reality. You have a thorough appreciation of the importance of the ones who contribute to your life experience. They help you see a brighter, stronger, more complete version of yourself when you look in the mirror. And you can do that for them too.

Okay, pause time is over. Moving on.

5. **Get curious about similar words within your rings.** What traits do your inner-circle members have in common?

Examine these traits more closely. Using the examples above, you might notice the words trustworthy, accepting, honest, and kind appear in both rings. No surprise. Those are inner-circle worthy traits. Would you want deceitful, judgmental, and mean personalities close to you? No way.

TRUSTWORTHY
ACCEPTING
HONEST
KIND

These traits are likely ones you highly value or see in yourself too. Feelings of personal gratitude may be kicking in right about now. That's a good thing.

What will you do next? That's up to you. You might choose to reach out to each friend or family member you thought about during this exercise. You might choose to schedule time with them to nourish both of your souls. You get the idea.

*Remember, cherishing your inner circle requires effort on your part. Take time to nurture the fulfilling reciprocal relationships in your life that make each of you happier, more content, and more accepting.*

## Ask

1. Has a notable life experience ever caused you to shift your perspective? What happened? How did the experience change your perspective?
2. Before you read this chapter, did you regularly nurture your inner circle? What will you do starting now to further cherish these important relationships in your life?

## SOLIDIFY WHAT YOU'VE LEARNED

◊ **LESSON 1:** Change course when a new path feels right.

◊ **LESSON 2:** Collect skills and confidence.

◊ **LESSON 3:** Let the strength of kindness flow through you.

◊ **LESSON 4:** Stay driven in the moment to excel under pressure.

◊ **LESSON 5:** Persevere with gratitude.

◊ **LESSON 6:** Redefine what accessibility means to you.

◊ **LESSON 7:** Choose to show up as the real you.

◊ **LESSON 8:** Trust yourself.

◊ **LESSON 9:** Cherish your inner circle.

## CHAPTER 10
# RENEW YOUR ENERGY

Has there ever been a time when you thought, *Now or never?*

One routine Monday morning, my eyes opened before the alarm rang. I peeled off the covers and sat up. Time to get moving with an early-morning caffeine boost.

Before heading downstairs, I threw on my cozy, gray hoodie sweater. Then I filled my large Halloween-themed mug with freshly brewed seasonal Starbucks® pumpkin spice flavored coffee.

Although the windows were closed, the air inside was crisp and cool. As I savored my first, steaming, cinnamon-infused sip, I looked outside at the changing leaves. While I watched dry yellow, orange, and brown leaves floating toward the ground, I felt like I was watching time tick forward as the season passed before my eyes.

Once the rest of the house started bustling, my thoughts drifted away like the fall leaves.

Onward. I continued with my morning routine. Coffee, workout. More hot coffee, designated computer time. This would require finding a quiet spot in our house.

During the fall of 2020, our kitchen had morphed into even more of a lively central hub than usual. The kitchen table had become a happening place because of the remote activities that occurred at home.

School. Work. Homework. Projects. Zooms.

This morning, I reserved a block of quiet time at our kitchen table "headquarters."

At this point, my attention was drawn to the unknown that lay before me. A career was important to me. However, it was not the most important thing to me. I knew I wanted a career where I could unapologetically be a happy mom, wife, and complete person with a fulfilling existence outside of work. That was who I had become.

It's possible, right? *Yes.*

I had gathered plenty of real career experience to know what a good fit felt like. A job where my exceptional, reliable performance was valued by secure, kind professionals instead of bringing out others' insecurities. A job where my trajectory was earned and supported instead of undermined behind the scenes. A job where shining was perceived as a good thing instead of dimmed by those who had a problem with it. A job where I could leave the office to attend family events or doctor appointments instead of "asking permission" ranked especially high on my list.

Is that too much to want? *No!*

By now, the wasted time and energy spent on past power positioning nonsense was irrelevant. I had thrown it all in my expanded learning experience bucket. What I hadn't thrown away was my desire to wake up to a fulfilling career.

Will I find what I seek to become the version of me I envision? *Yes!*

In 2020, unearthing the job I envisioned was like looking for a diamond in a field in the dark. By the time I arrived here, I absolutely knew something to my core: I would not sacrifice the life I wanted for the life someone else expected me to live. I was committed to finding the diamond.

As I scrolled through my messages, I spotted a potential fit in a consulting gig description someone had sent me. *This would be perfect*, I said to myself. It entailed a few months' commitment. On paper, it was a suitable blend of finance, operations, and strategy. Plus, there was little to no travel. No hesitation required on my part. Since I had to follow the formal application process, I started completing the information requested. So far, so good. Then I got to where it stated applicants must have a legal entity. I paused.

Taking a break, I stood, stretched, and walked around our kitchen. The hard, wooden kitchen chair was not exactly part of an ergonomic set-up.

Time to renew my energy. As I poured more ultra-hot coffee into my mug, I realized I was ready to pour my energy into creating the blissful life I knew was possible. I was ready to utilize my resources to advance my career.

As morbid as it may sound, I had the thought, *I've got things to do before I die.* Yet, reframing my decision in those terms was a game changer.

While the coffee mug warmed my hand and my heart, I resumed my seat at the kitchen table. Then I asked myself bluntly, "Do you want to create your own consulting business, yes or no?"

Sipping my Starbucks, I wholeheartedly decided yes; I wanted legal entity ownership as part of my career journey. I wasn't going to wait. I was ready to take a chance on what I wanted. Now.

*What's the worst that could happen?* I thought to myself. The answer was immediate. *Not giving it a go.*

I felt an immense sensation of zeal, which confirmed I was heading where I belonged. That same day, the legal entity JLM & Associates Consulting, LLC was formed.

Next, I completed the consulting job application I had started earlier in the day as a legal entity owner. I pressed down firmly on the submit button.

That evening, my supportive husband and I poured some cabernet sauvignon to share a celebratory toast at our kitchen table. I'll treasure that exuberant clink of our tall, stemmed glasses forever.

## **Reflect**

The leaves weren't the only things changing. The next morning, what jolted me more than my morning coffee, in a natural, energizing caffeine-free way, was my decision to become an entrepreneur.

In that one job description, on that one day, I saw a path to the life I wanted. I was open and ready. I was primed to refocus on my career, and I was open to doing so in accordance with *my requirements*.

I did pause. I did think. I didn't overthink. I didn't let guests like "what if this" or "what if that" or "you should" sit down at the kitchen table with me. They weren't invited.

As I reviewed what I had (and hadn't) done before reaching my inaugural entrepreneurial decision, clarity struck, revealing the important lesson I needed to absorb.

**Stop overthinking and get going.**

Right there at our kitchen table, I relied on my decision-making ability. I didn't analyze the situation upside down and sideways. I didn't start researching. I didn't ruminate or vacillate. I didn't prepare an analysis or presentation. I let myself go (in a good way) to become an evolved professional living as a whole person. I accomplished this while wearing cute sneakers and faded blue jeans, comfortable in my own skin, in our warm home on an autumn day.

What else? *Maybe*, *later*, or *we'll see* thoughts did not slow me down. I acted right then and there. I got going on my future.

As I reflected on this new development, I recalled Grandma Ann's soft voice, transmitting tranquil energy. "What is meant to be will be." Throughout my life, she encouraged me to allow things to unfold. Suddenly, I saw how this personal discovery was an extension of her earlier nurturing presence in my childhood. Things play out in due time. Imagining her sweet smile, I smiled too.

> **The more you let go, the more you become a match for what you desire.**

This lesson was a turning point in my career and personal life that remains relevant to this day. The moment I rose from bed that autumn morning, I knew I was in control of who I would become. When I decided to create a legal entity, I *felt* the harmonious satisfaction of making a significant decision in the absence of unnecessary overthinking. The more you let go, the more you become a match for what you desire.

When we are open to possibilities as the executor of our lives, we can grow into our best selves. If I had read that job description through a negative or unsure lens of no, can't, won't, maybe, later, what if, or should, I would have passed on an opportunity to embark on a fresh entrepreneurial journey. I would never have noticed the chance, let alone captured it.

Although this teaching came to me through a job application, it is about much more than a role or a career. That day, I knew *now* was the right answer. This is an example of how one event, one decision, one moment can alter your life.

So why did I choose to share this story? We've all experienced the jolt of renewed energy when we finally get out of our own heads and out of our own ways. Our overthinking patterns are on display decades before we get a handle on the real problem. Recall your teenage years when you may have over-hesitated about pursuing your crush, trying out for a new sports team, auditioning for a play, succumbing to peer pressure, or persevering toward your college dreams.

Later, as a professional adult, you're dealing with strings of daily decisions that can trigger too much thought. Some choices are far more impactful on your success outcomes than others. Some require courageous leaps of faith. For example, think back to when you became an entrepreneur.

What prompted you to take the chance? How did you know it was time to go all in?

When you extricate unnecessary overthinking and ruminating, you renew your energy. This renewed energy allows you to redirect your resources to believing you can instead of flooding your mind with reasons you can't.

The catch is to be open, present enough to spot what you want when it appears, and act to seize it. Let's learn how to renew your energy so you can stop overthinking and start accomplishing more.

## Learn

Overthinking happens. You have a brain, thoughts, and a business to run. Scrutinizing goes wild when those things get twisted, tangled, and tired.

It's okay.

If you are a thinker or analytical type, it's sure to happen. In fact, while I was writing this chapter, a special inner circle someone gave me a sticker that said, "Hold on. Let me overthink this." It was, in part, serendipitous. However, it served as a reminder to overthink less.

This is a challenging lesson to absorb, which is why it's in Chapter 10. You had to uncover the nine diamonds before this one to be ready to receive the tenth one now. Let's get right to it.

By now, it's clear you yearn for a more fulfilling life.

You know it's possible.

You covet something more, to become more.

You've identified something you want to pursue.

You're ready to take responsibility for brightening your future.

*So, what's the problem?*

You think too much.

There is "normal" thinking. Then there is that whole other debilitating dwelling land where you get yourself caught in a wearisome mental loop of overanalyzing:

*What if it doesn't work out?*
*What if I fail?*
*What if it's too much?*
*What if I lose money?*
*What will others say?*

*Am I too old/young?*
*Should I do this?*
*Should I wait?*
*Maybe I need more time.*
*Maybe later.*
*Maybe I should ask for some opinions.*
*I'll see.*
*I'm not ready.*
*I won't succeed.*
*It's too much change.*

Do you see yourself in any of that?

Overthinking isn't just about business or personal decisions. Sometimes it's about why something happened, what someone really meant by what was said, or what others think about you.

Even if you made a mistake that you can't stop reliving in your mind, let it go. What's done is done.

Other times, prosperity guilt starts creeping in, telling you you're self-centered or self-serving for wanting more. If to some becoming your best self means you're perceived as selfish, so be it. The ones who want to keep you in your place aren't secure in theirs. You're learning how to please yourself, not them, so who are really the selfish ones?

While you're spinning around your self-created wheel of woes like a harried hamster, all you're accomplishing is fatigue and dizziness. What good will come from that? You can't lead anyone, including yourself, when you're in a tiring tizzy.

Now what?

Since you're trying to live your best life, you need to redirect your mental resources accordingly. You do not need to rely on distracting external inputs, opinions, or voices. You are perceptive and competent.

Stop overthinking and get going. This concept appears straightforward. However, *knowing* you can renew your energy by shifting it from thought to action is far different than *doing* it. Acting instead of thinking about acting leads to different results, which is why this lesson is so critical. Action is the point of entry for the happiness you want to flow through your existence, which enables you to become who you envision.

At times, it's so simple to make massive decisions that amplify your life that you don't even realize how far you've just propelled yourself forward. Other times, you wrap yourself in your overthinking like a comforting security blanket.

It's time to toss that blanket. You don't need it. It's keeping you hidden instead of empowering you to lead your life in a new way.

What do you need? LTY.

LTY will let you know when doing more means doing less by simplifying your approach. You can simplify your thought process to configure your life with clarity. The times when you employ your independent, solid judgment to make the best decision for yourself are the times when you are clear-minded.

For example, let's say your business reaches the point where adding a team member could make sense. You vacillate, ruminate, and procrastinate. Six months pass. All you did was overthink the decision and no actions were taken.

Instead, stop overthinking. Ask yourself, *What do I need to decide?* Simplify your decision by breaking down the big question into simple yes or no questions:

Do I have enough work to keep another team member busy? *Yes.* (LTY gave you this answer immediately.)

What is a reasonable and competitive rate for a team member experienced in what my business requires? *Quick research reveals $XX per hour.*

Can my business afford that? *Yes, if I set an hourly budget per month.*

Where can I find the best candidates for my budget? *I remember a colleague recently hired a new team member with this expertise—I'll ask for some recommendations.*

Now your tasks become more straightforward and easier to complete.

If you used this approach during those same six months, you could have seized an opportunity rather than wasted it.

If you LTY, you know when you're ready to take a leap. In that decision-making moment, you know the only air you need to breathe is your own. You know the only judgment you need is yours. You know the only moment you need to feel is the one you are living right now.

LTY will guide you to renew your energy. Your personal and professional growth depends on it.

## Apply

No one makes you think too much. You do that to yourself. You can also stop it. Commit to act.

> **Stop being an impediment to your own prosperity.**

You can begin by enacting a few minor behavior modifications without changing the real you. Let's stop thinking and get going by instituting a new set of "rules" to help renew your energy:

1. **Eliminate certain words from your vocabulary.** You choose your words. There are things that don't need to be said or even thought. Certain words inherently trigger unhelpful overthinking patterns. You can stop using these words right now. It doesn't matter if the thought containing these words is important or unimportant; it's the impact on your thought patterns that counts.

   - *Should:* Do you tell yourself "I should" or others "you should"? Any sentence or phrase that includes the word "should" does not need to be said.
   - *Can't:* Do you want someone on your team who says and thinks in terms of "I can't"? Didn't think so. Don't be that person.
   - *What if:* What if the world implodes? You get the point. Cut that out.
   - *Maybe:* When you say "maybe," what do you mean? If you are saying "maybe" to avoid saying "I don't know," then say, "I don't

know." If you are saying "maybe" to avoid saying no, then say no. If you're leaning toward yes, then say yes. Say what you mean (without offending others) instead of talking in riddles.

It's quite something when you hear all four of these words strung together. Here's a common hypothetical.

I *should* hire another team member. But *I can't* find the right person. *What if* someone quits before I onboard a new employee? *Maybe* I'll be able to afford more options next year.

In this example, what got accomplished? Nothing. Was the outcome successful? No. Is the thought process positive? No. Do you hear the doubt? Yes. Is the probability high that the business owner is mentally drained? Yes. The business owner thinks they are thinking through the issue. Meanwhile, they are the impediment.

To illustrate the power of our words, here's the revised hypothetical.

I *will* hire another team member within the next six months. Although it's challenging to retain talent, I know I'm searching in the right places this time. In the meantime, I'm going to supplement with part-time, temporary help as a buffer for the next sixty days.

Do you hear (and feel) the difference? By erasing should, can't, what if, and maybe from your jargon, you are already on your way to taking control of your words, renewing your energy, and enhancing your well-being.

2. **Pinpoint when you're slipping into overthinking.** It's easy to let yourself get sucked into over-scrutinize mode as you're faced with decisions, situations, and relationships. For example, let's say a client said something yesterday that didn't sit quite right with you for whatever reason. Here you are today, on a mind tangent about what transpired. If you tend to overthink as a coping mechanism, you know what I mean. This is when you need to swoop into your overactive mind and flip the off switch. If you don't, you will continue wasting your resources on something in the past. You can't change what happened. However, you can prevent yourself from repetitive slipping injuries.

Let's pause for some simple math. Yes, math. Stay with me here; you'll see the importance in a minute. Assume on average that your overthinking "habit" consumes about an hour a day. This is realistic. It's also light considering those days your thoughts go on and on.

Well, one hour per day for an entire year is 365 hours. That's a lot of hours.

Now, divide 365 hours by twenty-four hours per day. *That equals fifteen entire twenty-four-hour days.* That's a lot of days to waste. What could you have been doing to enjoy those 365 hours, or fifteen days? Are you ready to stop being a jerk to yourself?

Even after you grasp this math problem, stopping yourself takes dedicated practice. Simplify it for yourself by acknowledging what popped into your mind. After all, you have feelings, memories, and thoughts. That's okay. What's not okay is when you and your loud mind chatter start sliding into excessive thinking patterns. That's not an attractive look.

Instead, tell your best self you aren't going there. If you slip, remind yourself not to go there again. You get the idea. You're not dismissing yourself or your feelings. By not wasting your energy on overthinking, you are preserving your resources for what matters most in your present and future.

3. **Use LTY as an asset.** Think of LTY as your central navigation system. Let's return to that question from the last section, "How do you know when LTY will impede your next step?"

   You may not like the answer. *It won't.*

   In other words, you must trust yourself.

   Let's review what LTY feels like. Keep in mind that LTY applies to *all* aspects of your life. The real you extends far beyond your business world.

   Have you ever made a solid decision in the absence of doubt, hesitation, or resistance? For example, look back to when you started a business, sold a business, designed a new product or service, moved to a new city, left a job that was worth leaving, went back to school, entered a great relationship, exited a bad relationship, or took a bucket-list trip.

Have you ever used your inner guidance system to help someone in your inner circle when they were distressed? Somehow, you knew what to say, when to say it, and how to say it.

Have you ever made a decision that almost felt "too easy?" When you got to the other side of the bridge you crossed, you looked back and realized how much ground you covered without realizing you were even walking.

In those instances, did you overthink, hesitate, or dwell?

Well, that's LTY. It didn't impede your next step. It helped you do something more than you could have done if you hadn't turned it on in the first place. You just may not have realized you turned it on.

*LTY allows you to gain clarity.* It does not cause you to over scrutinize or ruminate. It's also your kind and gentle friend in a harsh, complicated world filled with critics.

*LTY functions best when you keep it simple.* When you feel your mind wanting to rattle around, stop it. No rattling allowed. Focus. Keep your mental space clean and tidy to let LTY flourish.

Stop being an impediment to your own prosperity. LTY.

4. **Heed your speed.** Now that you're cleaning up your mental clutter, you're probably feeling more vital and clear-headed. As you envision your best path forward, execute with 100 percent effort. However, avoid executing with reckless haste.

   Let's stay here to talk business a bit.

   Walk with me through another hypothetical scenario. You decide to launch a business. You're so thrilled to be at the helm of your own business that you sink tens of thousands of dollars into marketing consultants, public relations, and "influencers" in hopes of raining revenue and recognition. The next thing you know, you've depleted your savings in less than a year. You realize your rash efforts were futile because you targeted the wrong demographic, the influencer didn't deliver, and the PR firm was full of more fluff than substance.

   What happened? You blew your hard-earned money because of your haste. You decided to pass go, which was a big leap forward.

# RENEW YOUR ENERGY

That was the good part. Then your vision got blurred by your eagerness. Not so good.

Now what? You remain committed to your business venture. However, you need to figure out how to clean up your mess. Good thing you are the enthusiastic, buoyant, and steadfast type.

This type of thing is avoidable when you LTY. You can get to where you want to go, knowing that taking one firm step at a time on solid ground is a reasonable course of action.

You're doing a lot of hard work. Let's practice honing your word choices to energize yourself to do and be more.

## Act: Word Find

## Word Find

```
W U E T L R K A Z U P Q P D U
M K X U Z S B U B B M A Y B E
S G Q E J N H T J L E A D A G
Y H A N H U P O J A M G H A E
L N Z D I T D K U G H E T M P
F X O K Z A R J N L B Y E Y A
N R Q N P C P I S W D D W T X
X N X X B I W X L M H Q I R I
Z S Y Y Q W K V K O S A L I F
D V F H F T E S U I D C T P T
M E W P A M Q I O O S G K I C
N R V A I J Y T U S C R J C F
B F W N A V C J T K W A W Q N
X G X E X W B O V G C O N M D
T L J N B F M Y J S F O M T R
```

Should    What If    Maybe    Can't

In the last section, we reviewed how vocabulary, thoughts, and outcomes tie together. This Word Find exercise will help you focus on the words you *choose* to use in the life you *choose* to live. It's also for the entrepreneurs out there who love a good brain teaser.

For this word find, you aren't searching for words on paper. You're searching for these words in your daily vocabulary:

- Should
- What if
- Maybe
- Can't

Once you commit to this exercise, it becomes a game, where the only person you're competing against is yourself. Who do you want to win: the overthinking, "never enough" version of yourself or the "commit to become more, LTY more" version of yourself? Whoever you allow to declare victory is up to you.

Here's how to get going:

- **Mentally note when you say the words should, what if, maybe, and can't.** For example, recognize that you used the word should two times in the last ten minutes. Imagine how many times you say it in an entire day? You get the idea.
- **Pay attention to when you use these words and what (or whom) you're referring to.** For example, are you referring to yourself, saying things like, "I should get to bed earlier during the week"? Or are you flinging these words at your inner circle or colleagues, using expressions like, "We should meet for lunch"? (Drop the should, schedule the lunch.) Or, "What if we start the project in January"? (Tell your colleague, "I am scheduling a new project to kick off mid-January.) Or, "I can't take on your project"? (Be more straightforward: you're currently booked, their budget is too low, or their needs don't align with your services.)
- **Mind your maybes.** The word *maybe* can be useful when you're not sure if something is true and you want to offer the possibility. For example, when connecting with others in writing or a presentation,

you may list several scenarios they "may" relate with, but you don't know for sure; you're offering possibilities. However, other times, the word *maybe* belongs in the trash, such as, "Maybe I'll go," when you have no intention of going. Tell the person you won't make it. Respect them by being honest.

With consistent word find practice, eventually these words won't roll off your tongue like they did before. Also, be patient with yourself. This new habit takes commitment and action. Eliminating the word *should* is the hardest.

*Remember, when your mind space is decluttered, you are more open and refreshed. Stop overthinking and use that energy to do more and be more, one firm, grounded step at a time.*

## Ask

1. Do you recall a time when you felt renewed energy? What triggered it? What changes did you experience before or after your energy boost?
2. How do you prevent yourself from overthinking?
3. Will you use different language after reading this chapter? How will you begin?

## SOLIDIFY WHAT YOU'VE LEARNED

◊ **LESSON 1:** Change course when a new path feels right.

◊ **LESSON 2:** Collect skills and confidence.

◊ **LESSON 3:** Let the strength of kindness flow through you.

◊ **LESSON 4:** Stay driven in the moment to excel under pressure.

◊ **LESSON 5:** Persevere with gratitude.

◊ **LESSON 6:** Redefine what accessibility means to you.

◊ **LESSON 7:** Choose to show up as the real you.

◊ **LESSON 8:** Trust yourself.

◊ **LESSON 9:** Cherish your inner circle.

◊ **LESSON 10:** Stop overthinking and get going.

# PART FIVE
# CHANGE: TRANSFORM YOUR EXPERIENCE

Do you feel more aligned with your wants and needs?

In Part Four, you focused on cocreating the life you envision with yourself and others. You allowed yourself to feel your emotions, trusted yourself more, and practiced patience. Then you shifted your perspective to cherish your inner circle. Finally, you figured out that you can renew your energy when you stop overthinking and get going.

While doing this work that no one can do for you, you discovered that the more you let go of what is not aligned with the real you, the more you become a match for what you desire.

Now you've arrived at the final part: change. Now that the sun—your spirit—is shining, it's time to elevate your life experience. As business owners, you are the ones to create the changes you need and navigate them to see the transformation through. Your business (and personal) growth relies on it.

Let's begin by learning how you can be your own catalyst for change.

## CHAPTER 11
# BE YOUR CATALYST FOR CHANGE

Has there ever been a time when you thought, *There must be a better way to do this?*

As I reviewed my calendar for the week, tension pulsed through my head, neck, and shoulders. By this point, the feeling was too familiar, too prolonged, and too much. I could feel the knots as I massaged the sides of my tight neck. I had already reeled in my priorities, accessibility, and distractions. This seemed to be a different issue.

I let out a heavy sigh that got my attention. *What is bothering me?*

Then I saw the answer staring right back at me. I was transfixed. Although my work calendar was full, it was structured in a way that was wasting time. That realization is enough to make any business owner sigh out loud.

I had this out-of-body experience, where I thought to myself, *How did I get to this point? Aren't I running my own business and my own calendar?*

I help clients solve business issues strategically. However, here I was in front of my calendar filled with appointments lacking strategic arrangement of meeting type, location, or day. I was also spending time on some commitments that best be eliminated. I was running my business while running myself ragged.

After unveiling my pain points, it was time for a fresh start. *Right now.* No overthinking or dwelling or delaying.

Somehow, my desires and actions had aligned about twelve hours before, without me realizing it. I had canceled a couple of appointments that felt out of sync. My intuition had sensed I needed clear space to enact positive changes in my daily life. *Was it LTY?* I felt my heart leap with excitement at solving this business calendar puzzle. My burden was lifting.

Anticipating an imminent intense problem-solving session, I opted for a healthy walk with Penny and Rockie to clear my mind space. Time in nature with my dogs was my sanctuary. The rhythm of planting one foot in front of the other in harmony with their paws doing the same is how I hit my reset button.

As Rockie's long, fluffy, apricot tail rocked back and forth and Penny's soft, pointy, brown ears danced up and down, I marveled at their innate ability to live in the present. They ambled along, enjoying smells in the air, sniffs in the grass, sounds of passing vehicles, noises of the neighborhood, and sights of other animals and humans. They were happy to saunter in sunshine, clouds, rain, snow, and wind. They were happy to be happy.

When I walk the dogs, I don't let them zigzag me all over the place. So why was I willing to zigzag from here to there for a business I own?

As I headed home at a brisk pace, with refueled creativity and dopamine, I, too, felt happy to be happy. I knew I couldn't move forward carrying the energy of old ways.

I dashed inside our house as a woman on a mission. Leashes off. Sneakers off. The mere promise of transforming my schedule to give myself more meaningful time lit me up.

To help me focus during my digital date with my calendar inefficiencies, I pulled my hair up high into a scrunchie bun—a "concentration" position. I grabbed a studious, sharpened number two pencil and yellow sticky notes. Then I sat down with my laptop, a fresh cup of coffee, and two tired dogs at my feet. I set my timer for thirty minutes as I went into efficient transformation mode, spotting patterns and identifying problems before formulating solutions.

Within five minutes, I had reformulated my approach to unruly meetings. Some of the in-person meetings could be virtual. Some of the virtual meetings could be phone calls or emails. Some meetings didn't require my participation at all.

Then I zoomed in on the in-person meeting and event demands. This part took a bit longer. I added up the actual time sacrificed by attending an in-person event thirty minutes away, factoring in driving time, getting "dressed well" time, exchanging pleasantries time, and adding traffic time. That one hour meeting easily takes at least two hours. I flagged in-person undertakings for further consideration.

As I scrolled through calendar weeks, there wasn't a reserved workday or part of one set day with no commitments. With discipline, that would be an easy fix.

I smiled when I saw my writing time was blocked out regularly. This signaled to me that I had prioritized my writing passion. That was on the right track. *Okay, great,* I thought. *How can I get my calendar on track to save myself time?*

By changing it. I put my mind to pen and paper to sketch out my desired weekly structure. Being a numbers person, I challenged myself to figure out the time savings between my current state and future state. So part of my creation entailed tracking my improvements for the next three months (I'll share my findings in a bit).

Presto! My timer sounded, signaling my thirty minutes were up. I knew what I needed to do.

## Reflect

Finding, fixing, and transforming clients' pain points can be exhilarating. Finding and fixing my own pain points to create what I wanted was a whole new level of exhilarating.

Leading up to the thrill of this workday transformation, my awareness about time constraints was dialed in. I felt compelled to start maximizing my time, which had entailed choosing to show up as the real me, building trust with myself, and cherishing my inner circle. I had learned to renew my energy and to stop overthinking to get going.

However, on this day, something felt amiss. Fortunately, I had the clarity of mind to hit pause. When I viewed time as the vessel for the who, what, when, where, and how of my existence, the lesson emerged.

**Get strategic about your time.**

I needed to align my time with the real me and my business.

So why did I select this story to share with you? Because time is a resource you know is finite. There's no way around that. However, you may find yourself giving it away to others day after day. As a result, you get the crumbs of time you leave up for grabs. Depending on the stage of your life, that is your reality some days. Other days, you're giving too much time away to your own detriment. You also find yourself wasting minutes, hours, and days here and there. Then, emotions like guilt, regret, or shame creep in when you realize you wasted your time, and it was your choice.

> **Your time is yours to hold. Your time is yours to give. Your time is yours to enjoy.**

Minus the negative emotions, you're right. As a business owner, how you spend your time *is* up to you. Your time is yours to hold. Your time is yours to give. Your time is yours to enjoy.

Earlier, I had focused on *who* I wanted to be in my career and personal life. That led to my realization about cherishing my inner circle. Now I was revamping *how* I wanted to safeguard my time in a strategic sense.

At this point in my life, this lesson is top of mind. If you wake up in the morning, then you are blessed to have time. What you do with that time is entirely up to you. It's easy to let it slip by.

You deserve to enjoy your experience. By focusing on the wellness benefits of claiming your time, your inner circle benefits from a happier you. Your customers benefit from a happier you. And *you* benefit from a happier you. You can become your own catalyst for change. Let's delve into how to get strategic about your time.

> **No part of being strategic about your time relies on external validation. It relies on you.**

## Learn

Time will slip by as the clock of life ticks. This is why it's so critical to hold your time now.

In the last chapter, you learned how to renew your energy to stop overthinking and get going. You practiced refining your vocabulary to reduce or eliminate use of the words *should*, *what if*, *I can't*, and *maybe*. Are you sticking with it? There's no place for that old energy when you are blooming to become your catalyst for the changes you want. Here's where you redeploy your renewed energy to optimize how you use your time.

*What's the problem now?*

You don't view time as something that you can optimize strategically.

*What's another problem?*

You may think you are being deliberate about how you spend your time.

*What else?*

You care what others think about you if you say no. (You're not overthinking anymore, remember?)

You *can* optimize your time strategically.

You *can* be more deliberate with your time.

You *can* focus on you to take back control of your time.

You've been collecting diamonds to prepare you for this strategic shift in the way you view, use, and protect your time. In Chapter 3, you discovered how kindness can flow through your business as a strength. You can be a kind giver *and* give in alignment with the real you. No part of being strategic about your time relies on external validation. It relies on you.

Then, in Chapter 6, you learned how to chill by redefining what accessibility means to you. At this point, you were deciding how to allocate your time, choosing when to grant access to others, and setting your level of personal privacy.

Now, you are focused on being deliberate about using your time. When you run a business, there are improvements you can make to hold more of your time in your pocket. Get strategic about getting strategic about your time. You're ready.

Speeding along in the essence of time, let's look at my time savings results during three consecutive months to illustrate how tactical time strategy can enhance your day.

Guess how many hours I saved in three months? Thirty-seven hours. Here's my time savings breakdown:

| Hours Saved | Action Implemented for Three Months |
| --- | --- |
| 9 | Changed virtual meetings to concise emails for a first-pass business compatibility screen. |
| 9 | Curtailed attending committee meetings and in-person and virtual networking events that weren't aligned with my business (and me). |
| 6 | Created virtual office time blocks to stack video meetings with short breaks between to reduce start and stop inefficiencies. |
| 5 | Revamped meetings. Scheduled video or phone calls instead of in-person for certain meetings. Used email instead of video or phone for meetings that didn't need to be meetings. |
| 5 | Grabbed hold of one day per week to enhance my workflow by organizing, planning, and acting. |
| 2 | Arranged meetings in the same geographical area with short breaks between to save driving time. |

| Hours Saved | Action Implemented for Three Months |
|---|---|
| 1 | Screened all meeting requests in advance. If the requestor didn't respond to my email or gave me the sense it was just going to be a sales call, I canceled the appointment. |
| 37 | **Total Sustainable Hours Saved in Three Months** (approximately 7 percent based on five eight-hour workdays per week for thirteen weeks) |

Dedicating thirty minutes to figure out how to save thirty-seven hours within three months is a good result. My study occurred within the first two years of launching my business. As a result, I was able to spend my sustainable time saved on more meaningful work, including gearing up for this book.

Anyone can get strategic about their time. The catch is you can talk all day about results; you must keep putting in the work to make it stick. So how do you apply this to your experience? Great question. This is addressed in the next section.

For now, consider the degree to which you claimed your time. Regardless of the type of business you lead, the stage of your business, or the current phase of your life, you are choosing how you spend your time. Even if you have an assistant or full team in place, you are still deciding where you are showing up and when.

To help you prepare for the next section, consider some questions:

- Do you feel like your calendar is causing you to carry a heavier mental load?
- Are you bouncing all around from here to there with starts and stops, causing breaks in your focus?
- Are you rushing or running late with frequency?
- Are you grouping appointments in a way that saves you or costs you time?
- Are you attending meetings, events, or conferences that leave you feeling uninspired?

- Are you participating in training sessions that aren't enhancing yours or your team's skills in fruitful ways?
- Are you looking at appointments on your calendar that don't mesh well with you or your business?
- Are you blocking out time for yourself to think, plan, organize, and create?

Okay, time's up.

## Apply

Become the catalyst for the changes you want, starting with getting strategic about your time. You can grab hold of your time, alleviate extra mental load, and help yourself find some peace by applying these three simple steps:

1. **Look for inefficiencies in your calendar.** Schedule thirty uninterrupted minutes to study your calendar more than you have before. This is not a task for you to delegate. You need to understand what you're dealing with before you can transform it.

   Look for inefficiencies in your schedule for the upcoming weeks. Take notes. Some areas to examine include:

   - *Scheduled time:* Are you overscheduled? Are you bouncing all over the place? Is your calendar organized?
   - *Gaps of time:* Do you have breaks between appointments? How long are the breaks? What do you do during that time? What could you do during the blocks of time between appointments?
   - *Meetings, conferences, events, training time:* Does your business require you to lead or attend in-person or video activities to stay abreast of trends, develop new business, expand your network, or advance your skills? Is the time, including getting to and from the events, reserved on your calendar?

- *Travel time:* Do you travel for work? Is it blocked out? Are your travel days well organized to the extent they are within your control?
- *Unscheduled tasks:* Are you dedicating chunks of time to work that isn't scheduled or even prioritized?
- *Wasted time:* What work could you eliminate (not delegate) without missing it?
- *Routine:* Do you perform certain tasks on certain days? Are they scheduled?

Remember, you are the catalyst for the changes that will enhance your experience. LTY. You will find something that is worth a second glance.

2. **Get strategic about what you want.** Do you recall the ALD approach from Chapter 6 for simplifying how to decide who gets access to your time and energy? You learned to view access in terms of all access (A), limited access (L), and denied access (D). You will apply ALD again here.

Based on your calendar findings, are you limiting and denying access in sensible ways? For example, are you reserving time for folks that are Ds? Or too much time for those who are Ls? Granting too much access can eat up chunks of your day to the detriment of your sanity, profit, and well-being.

A professional, skilled CEO has a strong hold on access. For example, based on my firsthand observations, you don't prance into a CEO's office unannounced, expecting undivided, immediate attention. Also, a strategic CEO meets and leads with intention while exercising a strong hold on time allotments. When a meeting time is up, it's up. They don't want to hear about added agenda items they weren't prepared to discuss.

Overall, they don't waste time. They have places to be. They have priorities. They have businesses to run.

You do too. So be the CEO. As the CEO of your business, how can you get strategic about your time?

- Do you want a dedicated block of time to plan for the following week?
- Do you want to travel more? Less?
- Do you want to get more stringent about your practical application of the ALD approach?
- Do you want a routine time to meet with your team?
- Do you want to block out a routine day and time for your administrative responsibilities?
- Do you want lighter or no appointments on a certain workday?
- Do you want fewer gaps between appointments?
- Do you want your appointments prescreened?
- Do you want fewer meetings?

Getting strategic about your time starts with realizing how quickly minutes add up to significant chunks of your life. Inefficient minutes turn into days, which turn into weeks of wasted time that you will never recoup.

Let's walk through a realistic example. You find you have excess space between meetings that occur on the same day at the same location or virtually. For instance, you have about thirty minutes between meetings twice per day. These are meetings that mesh well with you and your business, so the meetings do belong in your schedule. However, the thirty-minute break ends up wasted because you don't have time to start and finish anything. You piddle it away, checking social media or texting or doing something else you don't need to be doing.

Between meetings, you require five minutes for a bio break. So you waste twenty-five minutes, twice per day, in a five-day workweek. This means you lose fifty minutes per day, or a little more than four hours per week. For simple illustrative purposes, say you work forty-eight weeks per year; this translates to about 200 hours per year.

Now divide 200 hours by eight hours per average workday. *This equals twenty-five entire eight-hour workdays.* That's a lot of days to waste. What would you have rather been doing with that time?

Do you see how the minutes matter? Sit with your thoughts. Take notes.

3. **Transform how you spend your time.** What did your calendar study reveal about how you spend your time? How much time can you save?

It's common to find that you have been running around making yourself crazy while wasting time. You keep running, thinking you are efficient. After all, doesn't running around mean you're a busy business owner? Isn't that how it's supposed to be? No. And no.

Since you've been zigzagging all over the place to run your business, you may not have gotten this intimate with your calendar until now. That's okay. Regardless of your findings, be gentle with yourself. You're not overthinking anymore, remember?

You can keep an eye on your business and an eye on the clock. You can also work with the clock instead of against it. You saw earlier that increments of time that seem small on one day add up to big blocks of time after many days.

Now for the fun part. You get to create a general workday structure that you want while being strategic about your time. Based on what you discovered in steps one and two, what do you want to change with respect to how you spend your workdays?

Let's return to meetings as an example. Business meetings happen with customers, prospective clients, vendors, suppliers, your team, or all of the above. Then there are the industry events, training, committees, or volunteer work in which you may participate. You don't need to do it all. You also don't need to do it all in person.

Take each meeting on a case-by-case basis to make the best use of your time while growing your business. There is value in conducting business face-to-face. It depends on the situation. Keep in mind, when you are being strategic about your time, you choose when and where to show your face in person. Minutes matter.

Some meetings are best in person. You choose.
Some in-person meetings can be efficient virtually. You choose.
Some remote meetings can be conducted via phone. You choose.
Some meetings can be a concise email. You choose.

Also, consider the opportunity cost of your time. For example, let's say you devoted an entire workday of your time attending a conference, including an hour of driving time. The event was good, not great. Although you made a few new connections, you conclude that the probability of a new business opportunity is low. What else could you have accomplished during that day? Could you have met with prospective clients? Finished your next client pitch or presentation? Started the next chapter of your book? Met an inner circle member for lunch? Organized your messy house? You get the idea.

The next time a similar situation arises, you may pass to be strategic about your time. Also, what is the point in going to an optional meeting if you don't want to be there? Or if you show up scatterbrained because of what it entailed for you to get there?

Now that you know where you are losing time, design what you want in a way that works for you and your business. How will you reallocate the time you saved?

Let's focus on the keystone that matters most in your day, week, year, and life.

## Act: The Keystone

The unique keystone of your business is you. You must stay strong as the most important stone at the top of your arch, in this case, your life.

The keystone of your calendar is your time to work on your business without anyone else around. Keep in mind your keystone time is separate from the Silence Solution time we covered in Chapter 6, for you to you spend alone, not working, to collect your thoughts for the day. This keystone is the most important part of your weekly work schedule. If you find time to reallocate, this is the place.

Setting aside focused time alone to work on your business is an essential stamina-builder. It supports all the other moves you make that week. It supports your clarity as you choose opportunities to pursue. It supports the success of your outcomes.

This exercise will help you create a weekly calendar keystone as a first step to building your schedule and being strategic about your time. You will use your calendar keystone to do the following:

- *Think* creatively.
- *Plan* your week, month, and year. For example, in the last quarter of the year, you can block additional time to plan for the first half of the following year. Planning time is required for budgeting, business development, marketing, and creating.
- *Organize* what you need and when for clients, events, appointments, supplies, inventory, budgeting, marketing, and banking. Send follow-up emails or confirmations that require your direct involvement.
- *Create* what you planned. This could include fresh service offerings, social media posts, blogs, marketing materials, new training curriculum, event plans, presentations, or business pitches.
- *Do* the work you need to accomplish yourself, in peace and quiet. This is anything that requires you to focus, with zero interruptions.
- *Breathe.* Stay strategic by considering your new, transformed, strategic schedule you worked on in the last section.

Now set your weekly keystone.

What block of time per week will you set aside to do what only you can do for your business?

You can block out one longer session per week or two sessions per week. You choose what will work best for you, based on your personality and business. Some choose Fridays to plan for the following week. Some prefer the first day of the work week, which varies based on your business. Others prefer midweek.

As you consider where to set this weekly keystone, select times when you can have peace. Your office is quiet. Your team is not in the same place as you. Your significant other is at work. Your kids are out of the house. Your dogs are asleep. Your phone is put aside for emergency use. You get the idea.

When is your calendar keystone? Schedule this time to support the rest of your week, months, and year.

Make it happen.

| | **WEEKLY CALENDAR** ||||||||
|---|---|---|---|---|---|---|---|
| | **SUN** | **MON** | **TUE** | **WED** | **THU** | **FRI** | **SAT** |
| 6 am | | | | | | | |
| 7 am | | | | | | | |
| 9 am | | | | | | | |
| 10 am | | | | | | | |
| 11 am | | | | | | | |
| noon | | | | | | | |
| 1 pm | | | | | | | |
| 2 pm | | | | | | | |
| 3 pm | | | | | | | |
| 4 pm | | | | | | | |
| 5 pm | | | | | | | |
| 6 pm | | | | | | | |
| 7 pm | | | | | | | |
| 8 pm | | | | | | | |
| 9 pm | | | | | | | |
| 10 pm | | | | | | | |

Then play around with your new calendar. Test it out. Make necessary adjustments. Stick with it for sustainable transformation.

You're creating lasting change for yourself, which is a challenging feat filled with opportunity.

*Remember, stay strategic about your time.*

## Ask

1. Are you aware when you are wasting your time? What is your biggest time suck? How do you prevent yourself from wasting time?
2. After reading this chapter, how will you get more strategic about your time?

## SOLIDIFY WHAT YOU'VE LEARNED

◊ **LESSON 1:** Change course when a new path feels right.

◊ **LESSON 2:** Collect skills and confidence.

◊ **LESSON 3:** Let the strength of kindness flow through you.

◊ **LESSON 4:** Stay driven in the moment to excel under pressure.

◊ **LESSON 5:** Persevere with gratitude.

◊ **LESSON 6:** Redefine what accessibility means to you.

◊ **LESSON 7:** Choose to show up as the real you.

◊ **LESSON 8:** Trust yourself.

◊ **LESSON 9:** Cherish your inner circle.

◊ **LESSON 10:** Stop overthinking and get going.

◊ **LESSON 11:** Get strategic about your time.

## CHAPTER 12
# STOP TRYING TO DO IT ALL

Have you ever felt unsure about how to help yourself?

In the middle of the night, I lay in bed, staring at the ceiling. Covers on, covers off, flip right, flip left, pillow this way, pillow that way.

Tossing. Turning. Awake.

I tried fluffing the pillow as if it would make a difference. It didn't.

Earlier that night, I had spent a few solid hours on administrative work, including bookkeeping. I had been so consumed by so much that the important work that seemed unimportant had been piling up.

Although I had dug myself out from under that work task pile, its aftermath churned in my mind, cocktailed with my long list of tasks, to-dos, and priorities for my business. I felt tired and wired, simultaneously. Caffeine wasn't keeping me up. Feeling like I had too much to do by myself was keeping me up.

Counting sheep, dogs, or stars may have worked when I was a kid. But my founder life felt far from a storybook tale. The only images I saw when I closed my eyes were yellow and pink Post-it® Notes, not exactly as soothing as sheep.

Tossing. Turning. Still awake. Then the internal dialogue commenced.

"Why had I felt so compelled to give up my Friday night to get caught up on administrative work?" *Because you knew it had to get done.*

"On a Friday night, Jen, for real?" *Yes, Jen, for real.*

"Why am I wired this way?" *You like to get stuff done. It's part of the real you.*

Tossing. Turning. Still awake. The thoughts kept coming.

"Well, I want to change the way I'm wired." *You can't. Stop resisting it.*

"Then what can I change?" *Your approach.*

"Is this the sexy life of a founder?" *Right now, yes. This is the behind-the-scenes reality of it all. Accept it.*

Looking at the clock reminded me that time was moving forward. Meanwhile, I wasn't sleeping, resting, or accomplishing anything.

P.m. turned into a.m. I was literally watching time evaporate, adding to my angst. Feeling like I was having some sort of question-and-answer session with an angel, the internal dialogue continued,

"How do I stop trying to do it all?" *Figure it out. And remember, stop overthinking and get going.*

"When will this rough phase pass?" *It doesn't matter. You know it will.*

"How is this possibly going to renew my energy?" *LTY.*

"I need direction." *So direct yourself. LTY.*

At that point, I accepted the sleep loss. I got up.

My Saturday began around three in the morning with a "let's get on with it" kind of feeling. I felt like I had a hangover. Except it wasn't from a night of too much fun. It was the after-effect of choosing to give up a Friday night to work on my business. Then I gave up sleeping. Now I'm starting Saturday in the middle of the night, knowing I am already running on fumes.

This Saturday situation called for a different coffee mug. I got out my serious-sized "Go confidently in the direction of your dreams. Live the life you've imagined" mug to give myself the dire extra mental boost I needed.

At 3:15 in the morning, there I was, with my inspirational mug of fresh, steaming, black coffee, fuzzy slippers, Penny, Rockie, pink and yellow Post-it® Notes, and a pen ready for my Post-it® Notes pajama party.

## Reflect

My Post-it® Notes pajama party would no doubt help me pinpoint the problem. These notes help me organize my thoughts, priorities, and solutions. I use them daily, and I have for many years.

On a yellow note, I wrote, "Productivity." Then I sat with that.

I was admitting to myself that productivity was still an issue for me in some way (says the woman in fuzzy slippers hosting a Post-it® Notes pajama party before sunrise). I thought I had reeled in productivity enough to learn to chill (see Chapter 6). I *had* made progress. However, this pajama party proved to me that something remained amiss. There was another lesson for me to unveil.

Productivity was a learned behavior for me. Earlier in my career, productivity was a consulting metric that emphasized billable hours. I worked for companies where billable hours were required to be reported weekly. Anything below 90 percent for more than a few days was like receiving an F.

Plus, I like to rise early. I grew up in a house that was alive by sunrise with morning-person parents getting ready for work, the smell of fresh coffee, and a dog that would jump on my bed.

My productivity became a habit. Then it continued from my big business career to small business. To some extent, my desire to produce is part of the real me. However, I didn't need to do everything that I was doing myself.

So on another yellow note, I wrote, "Delegation."

Okay, now I was on to something.

Then I put the pink notes into use to signal something different, an impending change. I asked myself, "What are you ready to stop doing yourself right now?"

"Bookkeeping," I blurted out.

At that moment, the lesson arrived clear as day, even though it was still pitch-dark outside.

**Do what matters and delegate the rest.**

I needed to align what I did in a way that matters to the real me and my business. Being productive does not ensure operating with strategic purpose.

> **Trying to do it all is not a sustainable strategy.**

So, why did I share this story with you? Because that pajama party started out with me feeling out-of-sorts and ended with me renewing my energy. That night helped me see the big picture where time, delegation, performance, results, strategy, and change reside. It doesn't matter how self-sufficient you are or what kind of business you lead. Trying to do it all is not a sustainable strategy. I realized that staying productive wasn't the catch-all solution to getting work done. My productivity wasn't helping me focus on the work that mattered most, perform my best, or sleep well. I needed to alter my approach.

Earlier, I had focused on revamping *how* I wanted to safeguard my time in a strategic sense. Now I could choose what work matters most to me. I could also choose what could be delegated and how. What was I also choosing? Myself.

You *can* stop trying to do it all. Let's move on to how.

## Learn

You're ready to focus on doing what matters. You're ready to delegate what you don't need to do yourself. This is the link between being in control of your time and energy.

In Chapter 10, you redeployed your renewed energy to optimize how you use your time.

In the previous chapter, you became the catalyst for the changes you want and got strategic about your time. You focused on learning how to efficiently use your time and create a new schedule.

*So, what's the problem now?*

You are using nonrenewable time to do things you don't need to be doing yourself (or at all).

*Why?*

You think you can do it all. And you can, to a point. Then you get real with yourself.

*What's another problem?*

You have a mental block about paying someone to do work you can do. Get over it. Stop doing work you dread when you can afford to pay someone to do it so you can do more of what you love.

*What else?*

You think doing it all is part of the real you. Doing it all is not a self-sufficiency badge of honor with bragging rights. It is not a measure of your intelligence, worth, or value. To some extent, it becomes a measurement of your control issues and declining mental health. Let it go—to grow.

Are you a business owner still trying to do it all? Creating. Planning. Leading. Hiring. Running. Number crunching. This is not sustainable. This mode of operation causes stress, fatigue, frustration, and distraction.

Stop trying to do it all so you can redirect yourself toward meaningful achievements. You can succeed at what matters to you. You can run a business, go back to school, write a book, host a show or podcast, teach classes, deliver speeches, create a new product, launch a new service, design clothing, enjoy your family, or whatever else you desire. However, you don't need to do *all* the work for *all* those things yourself on top of *all* the other tasks you do daily.

Let's go back to my bookkeeping example. At the time, paying someone else to do my bookkeeping was not an option I was even exploring. I thought, *I know numbers. I'm organized. I'm good at stuff like this.* The later realization was it doesn't matter if I'm good at something. I don't have to do it forever. I also don't have to do it all.

Once I saw the change to make, I set a goal for myself that within sixty days, I would outsource my bookkeeping to a professional. I would maintain oversight without doing the nitty gritty.

As a business owner, it is imperative to know your numbers. It is critical to have a reliable bookkeeper. This person doesn't have to be you. It's okay to enlist support where needed. It does not mean you are weak. Hiring assistance doesn't mean you can't handle it. Delegation is a good thing. Think of delegating as streamlining your systems to give you more power.

Let's explore how you can execute delegation to elevate yourself.

## Apply

The ability to delegate effectively is a strength that means you are prioritizing the health of your professional and personal lives. The strength embedded in the strength is execution. Without execution, you can talk all day long about delegation, but it won't get done in a way that grows your business, if at all.

Develop your delegation and execution strengths by applying three simple steps:

1. **Choose strategically**. Before you can make delegation decisions, understand your current position. Then you can prioritize the work that makes the most sense to move to someone other than you.

   Right now, ask yourself these three questions:

   - What work do I love doing?
   - What work piles up?
   - What is my current monthly budget to spend on outsourcing work to anyone else?

   The purposeful work you love doing is worth doing yourself—for now. Currently, this is what matters the most to you. It is also worth keeping yourself at the helm of strategic decisions, collaborations, and new revenue generation. So let's explore your answer to number two by asking yourself:

   - Why is certain work accumulating?

- Could someone within my company do this work?
- Do I need expert help outside of my company?
- Do I need help with certain household jobs?

Let's go back to the bookkeeping example. Such tasks can accumulate if you have more important work that consistently moves the bookkeeping tasks to the bottom of your to-do list.

Another hypothetical example involves staffing inefficiencies and opportunities. You are aware you need to make changes. However, you don't have the financial acumen and time to prepare a strategic analysis to help you make advanced decisions. This means you are holding yourself back from increasing the profits and improving the workflow for your business next quarter. You require expert guidance outside of your company. Accept it.

As a result of this step, you may make a bonus discovery: you are doing some work you no longer need to do at all. Examples include social media marketing that isn't bringing you new business or sending elaborate holiday cards that you no longer enjoy. You get the idea. Give yourself permission to let go of work that no longer serves you.

Now let's address the essential money question. Today, how much could you afford to spend per month within your means to outsource work to someone else? Think in terms of monthly cash flow, without reliance on borrowed money (loan, credit card balance, etc.).

Remember, you are going through this strategic process to do more of what matters most to you *within your budget*.

2. **Execute.** Execution is critical. This is the difference between reaping the benefits of your strategic growth by scaling or continuing to tread water where you are today. For growth, think in purpose terms of customers, revenue, profit, and market presence.

    Here, you get strategic about being strategic, similar to how you got strategic about your time in the previous chapter. The process of execution involves taking time to prepare to execute. You decide what makes sense for you to delegate to someone else.

## ALIGN YOUR BUSINESS WITH THE REAL YOU

This work falls into two key categories:

- **High value to your business.** This category requires expert help outside of your company, such as a project or service you require from specialized talent to strengthen your strategic business foundation, expand your market presence, scale your business, or simply guide you in a way that elevates you and your business. Examples include large-scale product launch, high-quality financial and operational planning, business and strategic planning, coaching, training, brand marketing, publicity, and legal advisory. You require assistance for a period rather than an additional employee.

   At this point, focus on the help you need now rather than your future goals more than a year from now. Some of this work comes with lofty price tags. Although you may need certain services to lead your business with strategic purpose, you don't require the sports car turbo equivalent of some services. There are high-caliber providers that serve entrepreneurs in different business sizes and stages without a turbo price tag. You will find what you need. If you can't afford help in certain areas at this time, that's okay; you can revisit this later when your business is more profitable.
- **Low/medium value to your business**. This category is more task-oriented, such as bookkeeping, taking inventory, completing purchase orders, answering phones, scheduling appointments, and some marketing efforts. It can be delegated with low to medium effort. You're at the point where it doesn't make sense for you to be bogged down by this work anymore.

Keep in mind that your answers are not confined to only your business tasks. As a professional with work responsibilities, you will require help in your personal life too. When you own a business, the personal and professional are intertwined. You don't have time to do it all. You don't have to do it all. Stop trying to do it all.

You may need to outsource some home maintenance chores, including landscaping, home repairs, housecleaning, or dry cleaning.

As long as you can afford it and find someone you can trust, start small and simple:

- What is one work task you could delegate?
- What is one home task you could delegate?
- Do you have existing resources to do the work for you?
- Do you need to find an expert consultant or service provider to do the work?

Now you are ready to execute. Your deadline is to make it happen within your budget in the next sixty days.

Why a deadline? Because you need to hold yourself accountable to execution while moving your business forward.

Why sixty days? Because it gives you realistic time to find the right person, get them started, and refocus your attention on doing more of the work that matters to you. Thirty days may cause extra stress on you; ninety days isn't enough pressure on you to make it happen.

Are you following my logic?

So, what did you choose to delegate? To whom?

As a result, what work will you choose to focus on more?

3. **Follow through and follow up.** After you assign the task to your assignee, you're far from done. You are responsible for communicating with the person doing the work for you. This is the critical part that so many miss.

   As the CEO, you focus on results without wasting time. It's hard to focus on results if you lack an effective communication channel.

   Let's break it down into simple bite-sized pieces; when you hand off the work, here are the tasks you need to oversee:

   - **Define** measurable success criteria (begin with the end in mind).
   - **Communicate** the deliverable (show and tell your assignee what you want completed).
   - **Communicate** the due date (if you don't, it won't get done

efficiently; ask me how I know).
- **Communicate** the delegated authority (limit access to confidential information, limit authority to act on behalf of your company).
- **Manage** expectations (set milestones).
- **Monitor** (establish a follow-up system with the assignee that works for you).

Do you see the communication theme?

You get to choose to communicate in a way that suits you. After you delegate one piece of work, give it time to stick. Then, repeat the above three steps for another task, and so on.

It's common to feel like delegating is more of a headache than it's worth. However, the more you put it off, the more you are hindering your progress.

Isn't doing more of the work you love and less of what you dread appealing? Isn't this part of why you started your business in the first place? Wouldn't you rather spend time doing the work that you want to do rather than digging yourself out from a pile of work that keeps mounting—or isn't getting done at all?

You saw earlier that increments of time that seem small on one day add up to big blocks of time after many days. The same concept applies to the effective execution of delegation. Let's explore through an if/then lens.

## Act: If/Then

In the Chapter 2 exercise, you worked on "unpacking" the "what ifs" weighing you down. Then, in Chapter 10, you started to eliminate "what if" from your vocabulary as part of your effort to stop overthinking and get going.

Now, we are going to use "if" combined with "then" in a useful way to illustrate the cause-and-effect relationship between delegation and results.

The key assumptions are:

- Tasks delegated are within the monthly budget without incurring debt.
- Execution can occur within the sixty-day deadline mentioned in the section above.
- All the delegated activities save you time, which enables you to accomplish more of what you want.

To ensure you can delegate while staying within your monthly budget, start identifying ways you can save money and redirect it to outsourcing the work that makes the most sense for you to delegate. For example, saving a couple hundred dollars a month can help you offload a task, even if it's relatively small. Think of it this way: If I cancel the XYZ service that costs me $150 per month—that I'm not even using—I can put that cash toward paying for [fill in the blank]. Money savings that seem small at the time can elevate your daily life in significant ways. Redirect your flow.

Here are some examples:

## ALIGN YOUR BUSINESS WITH THE REAL YOU

| Life Area | If I Delegate This | Then I Can Do This |
|---|---|---|
| Work | Bookkeeping | Focus on work I love |
| Work | Strategic staffing analysis with revised budget and recommended action steps | Achieve the staffing schedule I want, a more cohesive team, and increased profit |
| Work | Front desk reception, including answering phones | Spend more time on paying clients, which will increase my bottom line |
| Personal | House cleaning | Be happier and more engaged on the weekends with my friends and family |
| Personal | Closet organization | Feel more organized, which renews my energy |

Now it's your turn. Complete the chart below based on the examples above and what you learned in this chapter. Then, determine how you can use this methodology to boost your desire to delegate and your ability to fully execute whatever you delegate.

What will you accomplish next?

| Life Area | If I Delegate This | Then I Can Do This |
|---|---|---|
| | | |
| | | |
| | | |
| | | |
| | | |

*Remember, just because you can do it all yourself doesn't mean you must.*

## Ask

1. Do you view delegation as an obstacle? Or do you delegate well? Do you follow through and follow up?
2. After reading this chapter, how will you pare down your workload to start doing what matters most? What will you delegate within the next sixty days?

## SOLIDIFY WHAT YOU'VE LEARNED

◊ **LESSON 1:** Change course when a new path feels right.

◊ **LESSON 2:** Collect skills and confidence.

◊ **LESSON 3:** Let the strength of kindness flow through you.

◊ **LESSON 4:** Stay driven in the moment to excel under pressure.

◊ **LESSON 5:** Persevere with gratitude.

◊ **LESSON 6:** Redefine what accessibility means to you.

◊ **LESSON 7:** Choose to show up as the real you.

◊ **LESSON 8:** Trust yourself.

◊ **LESSON 9:** Cherish your inner circle.

◊ **LESSON 10:** Stop overthinking and get going.

◊ **LESSON 11:** Get strategic about your time.

◊ **LESSON 12:** Do what matters most and delegate the rest.

## CHAPTER 13
# APPRECIATE THE REAL YOU

Have you ever felt in complete harmony with yourself and others around you?

Our curious brown eyes met. I noticed the long eyelashes, shiny walnut-colored hair, and tall, strong stature. We blinked simultaneously. I felt like we were communicating and connecting without a word.

All of a sudden, a fluffy, long-haired black cat with magical green eyes appeared at my feet. It gazed at me and circled my tall, charcoal-gray leather boots. This was one of those synchronous moments in life that garnered my immediate awareness. I couldn't help but think to myself that this striking creature was here to get my attention and convey a message about what I was about to learn so that I was ready to receive.

I felt grounded in spirit.

Then I smiled and whispered something sweet while placing my hand on a different strong, muscular shoulder beside me. I got in position, sat up straight, shoulders back and arms relaxed. I felt much taller.

There was no tension. There was natural ease. I was trusting myself. I sensed that the trust was mutual.

Now, it was time to learn something new and exciting. My calves gave a quick, positive hug as I said, "Walk." We began to walk forward. We turned right; we turned left. We practiced going and stopping. I was learning with a trainer who made me feel comfortable on this magnificent horse named Shelby.

Twelve years had passed since I had been up close and personal with a big horse like this. Career, motherhood, marriage, house, dogs, and other obligations all came first. Today, I came first. Thanks to LTY, I got in the saddle and in a new environment.

I was living in the present, immersed in every breath of the experience. It was only the three of us in a wide-open space. I was in horse heaven.

Noticing something different about the saddle, I asked my instructor about it. Although I had booked a Western lesson, here I was on an English saddle. I had no central horn to hold. I had never ridden English before. At this point, I would not have chosen English on my own. I found the humor in that it was chosen for me. Since I wasn't overanalyzing anything, I didn't realize it until after I was already in the saddle.

I also saw the underlying meaning after my instructor described the differences between the two riding styles. The English saddle is smaller, lighter, and more elegant, which requires more precise saddle balancing. This makes English more challenging for some. Overall, Western is known to be more stable and comfortable.

Message received.

*I must trust myself to provide my own stability and comfort.*

Next we practiced posting, when I learned how to rise up and down out of the saddle in rhythm with the horse's trot. I had to use my thigh muscles, not my calves, to rise from the saddle while the horse was moving forward. Quite challenging.

Horseback riding may look easy. It is not. Posting requires a ton of inner thigh strength, balance, and determination.

Up. Down. Up. Down. Up. Down. Up. Down. Up. Down.

The instructor and I shared a few good laughs. I didn't care how hard it was. I was loving every second of it.

Then my trainer got serious again. She literally said that I was going to hate her for what was next. She told me to take my right foot out of my stirrup. Then she told me to take my left foot out of my stirrup.

Finally, she told me to let go of the reins. The second she said that, I was in fine tune with the reason this was happening in my life.

There I was, sitting on a large horse, without holding on with my hands or my feet. The only thing between me and the horse was trust (and an English saddle).

Next, my trainer told me to post. I glanced at her quizzically. This took inner thigh strength to a whole other dimension, not to mention calm confidence. My trainer noticed I was trying to use my arms to help propel me up and balance. She instructed me somewhat sternly to stop that and to put my hands on my hips. I had a bit of a laughing fit. She laughed too.

Then I did it.

Up. Down. Up. Down. Up. Down. Up. Down. Up. Down.

I didn't get that far up, but I got up. It wasn't elegant, but I did far more than I expected.

The grand finale to my lesson concluded. It was time to dismount. I grabbed the middle of Shelby's mane, swung my right leg around, and slid slowly down the side of her big body. When I jumped to the ground, I realized how far up I had been, which was a really cool feeling.

*I did it.*

We walked my new horse friend back to her stall. I hugged her goodbye, pet her long mane, and said, "Thank you, Shelby." She looked at me, her big brown, tender eyes seeming to say, "You're welcome."

And when I turned to leave, the cat with the dazzling eyes that made it a point to greet me when I arrived was there. The immediate thought that came to me was that there is no external magic that will create success. I manifest what I want through my continued commitment to integrate my experiences, progress forward, and execute. Once I thought that to myself, the four-pawed feline sauntered outside.

I met a few of the other horses and a sweet pony. One of the lovable, solid-dark-brown horses showered my hands and arms with affectionate, tickling kisses. This was a first-ever horse kiss experience, which I will remember forever.

I felt so welcome, comfortable, and relaxed in this serene environment that I didn't want to let much time pass before I rode again. So I booked my next lesson to come back to this slice of horse heaven. While I exited the facility, the bright, warm autumn sun beamed down on me as I walked forward into my life.

## Reflect

I let it all soak in.

I sat in my car observing the majestic horses in the corrals in front of me as the sun penetrated the windows. I've always loved the palpable peacefulness of horses (and dogs). Simply being in their presence feels like a marvelous gift.

As I started the car engine, I smiled, thinking about all the spectacular little moments that day before my arrival at the equestrian center. I recalled the extra-long Rockie and Penny cuddles with my husband that morning; the robins who had a little early-morning party outside our bedroom window as I blow-dried my hair; and the friendly neighbor I conversed with while walking our dogs.

Then I replayed more memorable moments from the last few days leading up to this event. I recalled the productive work meeting where positive outcomes were discussed in a collaborative manner. I remembered three gorgeous, fluffy, bushy-tailed red foxes who hung out together in our backyard for a full ten minutes while my husband, son, and I all had the pleasure of observing. I shared this experience with some members of my inner circle who get that nature encounters boost my spirit.

My drive continued as the next memory came: the previous weekend's afternoon walk when Penny, Rockie, and I got caught in an absolute downpour, resulting in me enjoying the most invigorating, rain-drenched frolic ever, arriving home completely soaked and elated.

As I waited at a red traffic light, another memory appeared. The shoe girl within me recollected the unboxing of my riding boots. When

I tried them on again, I found the purchase receipt from September 2011. I had originally bought them for our family fall trip to Vermont when we visited a horse facility.

Since that trip, I had envisioned myself riding and being around horses. However, I hadn't made it a priority. Somehow, everything else became a priority. Besides, I worked way too much, overanalyzed way too much, and searched outside myself way too much. So my horse-riding vision was boxed up with the boots for twelve years.

Twelve years.

Until today.

I had arrived at the equestrian center appreciating the real me who was walking through the horse-and-hay-scent-filled entrance in her riding boots. I chose to arrive on a divine path in more ways than one. I felt it in my heart.

I arrived already feeling accomplished and centered. Then I connected with the new human and horse faces I met with kindness. During my lesson, there was zero resistance on my part. I wasn't riding against anything. I felt present. I felt engaged. I felt strong. I felt confident. I felt alive.

The real me who wore those boots again was no longer willing to keep her visions, wants, or needs in a box. After all, I had become an entrepreneur to create a path where I could live my best life.

After my horse adventure, I felt more fulfilled, knowing I was heading home to a warm, inviting, and supportive life built with the family (including Penny and Rockie) I love more than anything on earth. At that point, the lesson landed as clear as that afternoon's sun-filled, bright blue sky.

**Love your life.**

My horse experience unleashed positive internal reflections that continued into that evening. Later that night, I felt drawn to grab a keepsake gift from my bookshelf, the hardcover *Women Who Run with the Wolves* by Clarissa Pinkola Estés, PhD. I reread the inscription out loud, by myself:

Dear Jen,
For a young woman who already knows her inner strength. You've been a wonderful student, editor, and, most importantly, person to know and to work with. I wish you all of life's joys.

This graduation keepsake was a missing puzzle piece that had been sitting on a shelf, waiting for me to rediscover it at the right time (similar to those riding boots). This book was gifted to me from my high school AP English teacher, journalism teacher, and advisor for my high school's newspaper, for which I was co-editor-in-chief. She was a special human who shaped my life during those formative years.

Her inscription conveyed she thought I already knew my inner strength. Later, during adulthood, I questioned it at times. She taught me interpretation, communication, and writing skills that further developed throughout my life, culminating where I am right now.

Until this night, I had thought my journey toward becoming an author unfolded in phases that commenced with journaling in 2020, followed by blogging, which led to my creation of the JLM & Associates Consulting, LLC Enlightened Leadership Blog. Now I realized this journey was prepaved, in a sense, within the younger version of the real me decades before.

Over the years, some parts of me changed, and some parts of me stayed the same. My veterinarian visions gave way to business ambitions; my global work travels gave way to motherhood; my angst gave way to gratitude; my dark clothing gave way to a brighter wardrobe; my stilettos gave way to sneakers; my external searches gave way to internal trust; and my overthinking gave way to renewed energy. However, my desires for a loving family, trustworthy inner circle, kind strength, fulfilling career, and a meaningful, purpose-driven life remained intact as part of the real me.

I felt grateful for all of it.

At that moment, I realized I had achieved a richer understanding of my life. The younger version of me and the current version of me united in passion and purpose. I was far from where I'd been. Since then, almost without knowing it, I had transformed my own experience step by step.

So, why did I choose to share this story? Because it illustrates that loving your life starts with appreciating yourself. There is no map pointing you in the direction of loving your life. It can take decades to recognize some of your connected awakening moments, at which point you see that the real you was emerging all along, with your participation, even if you didn't realize it at the time.

When you reach the point in your life of truly recognizing and appreciating the real you as you are, then you can love your life to your core. Since I had turned my attention to my own goals, I was able to take an active stance in my life. Then I immersed myself in work and activities I love, which, on this day, included riding a horse. Of course, you don't need to get on a horse to understand this lesson.

> **As you learn to appreciate the real you, you'll be able to love—really love—your life.**

When you appreciate the real you, you are accepting your whole journey, sprinkled with your mistakes, your failures, your struggles, your lessons, your obstacles, your pains, your discomforts, your values, your qualities, your goals, your needs, your health, your opportunities, your intentions, your confidences, your connections, your creations, and your spirit. And you can be grateful for all of it.

As you learn to appreciate the real you, you'll be able to love—really love—your life.

## Learn

Once you muster up your courage to enact the positive changes you want to create, there is no going back to the previous version of your life. However, you may end up connecting dots across decades, like I did, to form some surprising story connections.

At this point, you have emerged as a more elevated business owner who knows how to tap into your unique recollections, roles, responsibilities, resources, resilience, and relationships to influence the direction of your life. You worked through the first four of the 5Cs to:

1. **Connect** with yourself and others by listening to yourself.
2. **Clarify** your role in your journey.
3. **Control** your outcomes by taking charge of your life.
4. **Cocreate** the life you envision for yourself and with others.

You are still working on the fifth C—**change**—to transform your experience.

Overall, the ultimate goal is for you to love your life. Appreciating the real you *as you are* is the precursor for truly loving yourself and your life.

What do I mean by the real you?

The real you is a blend of life experiences past and present. The real you has traveled long distances for decades without a map. The real you traipsed through messy, heavy muck to get to where you are right now. The real you knows your true values, wants, needs, likes, and dislikes. The real you feels more at ease without trying to "fit in." The real you earned grit and humility. The real you values your inner circle. The real you holds abundance, inner wisdom, and personal power.

Some parts of the real you live within you from your past. Some parts slid away. Some parts changed. And some parts are still transforming.

Take a moment to appreciate how much you've achieved so far. What are some of the life-changing moments and accomplishments embedded in the real you?

As business owners, you devote resources to running your show and caring for so much outside of yourself. However, you also deserve to love your *entire* life, which is filled with true connections, harmony, and potential.

In reality, the idea of loving your life may provoke internal dialogue that sounds like this:

*Yeah, right. There's no such thing.*
*I'm happy (I think).*
*I try to act happy.*
*My life is good enough.*
*I have no time to love my life.*
*I work too much.*
*Today sucks.*
*This week/month/year sucks.*
*My life sucks.*
*I'm living the dream (said with sarcasm).*
*I don't have options.*
*I need more money to enjoy my life.*
*I don't know how much longer I can do this.*
*I just want to retire.*
*Things will be better when . . .*

We've all been there in one way or another. As we covered earlier, life throws us crises, curveballs, losses, distractions, and more. However, nothing good comes from dwelling on negatives. This perspective can be challenging at times when it feels easier to complain, dwell on, or deny.

Even though moments, days, months, and heck, years can be rough, the whole of your life isn't diminished. Loving your life is 100 percent a choice you make. No one can make you love your life. No one can force you to change your perspective. No one can "fix" your life.

If you feel like loving your life seems outlandish, then ask yourself, would you rather wake up every morning feeling alive or like a curmudgeon? The choice is yours.

Choose to feel alive. Your energy is best spent appreciating yourself and loving the life you can still wake up to every day. You'll also feel and look better. Plus, you'll be much more enjoyable to be around if you're upbeat. As much as your inner circle loves you, they prefer when you're cheerful (ask me how I know).

Let's focus on loving your life with *gratitude*.

## Apply

Since you are responsible for leading your life, you have lots of options. At this point, you are well resourced to define your personal and professional success in alignment with the real you. The aligned version of you can be yourself, be kind, be present, and be grateful.

How do you recognize when you're in alignment?

You *connect* with yourself.

You *listen* to yourself. *LTY.*

You *know* you are special, beautiful, and worthy.

You *accept* what happens.

You *allow* the strength of kindness to flow through you.

You *focus* on being present rather than ruminating, dwelling on, or overthinking.

You *create* what matters most to you.

You *appreciate* yourself, your inner circle, and your journey.

You *enjoy* the little moments as much as the big ones.

You *feel* grateful in your heart.

Okay, you appreciate the real you. How do you bring this appreciation into your overall experience and love your life more? You're getting there. Stay with me.

Just as you own the tool of LTY to access guidance at any time, you also own the tool of gratitude, which can help you love your life more at any time. Using this tool of gratitude doesn't cost you money. It also doesn't rely on anyone other than you. It simply requires clear-minded, focused energy. It also yields high returns by giving you a raise in more ways than one.

Let's revisit a part of Chapter 5, where you were introduced to my Gratitude Equation for those times in life you need dedicated effort and energy to pull yourself through. In that context, the Gratitude Equation helped you carve out space for yourself to accept what is, free yourself from unproductive thoughts, and focus on being grateful for what matters most.

As a refresher, here's the "math":

## APPRECIATE THE REAL YOU

> **The Gratitude Equation**

$$\textit{What Is Real} - \cancel{\textit{What Is Not Real}} + \textbf{Gratitude} = \textit{What Is with Gratitude}$$

However, now you are going to use "new" math for your everyday life:

> **The Gratitude Equation**™

$$\textit{What Is Real} + \textbf{Gratitude} = \textit{What Is with Gratitude}$$

This is how the real you, who appreciates the real you, loves your life more.

Now that you progressed with me to the final chapter appreciating the real you, you are going to use this version of this same tool from your new vantage point. You can use this tool whenever you want. You don't need to be pushing through a health crisis or some other tough challenge. Either version of the Gratitude Equation applies to any facet of your life.

What has changed in this equation? For the normal, daily life you love as the real you, there is no room for your doom-and-gloom, worst-case scenarios, or what you imagine others are thinking or saying about you. So "What Is Not Real" has been eliminated. The complete, real you needs, wants, and deserves to love your life without overthinking or unnecessary distractions.

Here are the three simple steps:

1. **What Is Real:** What Is Real includes what you know to be true about your life as the real you—the real you who can be kind, be a giver, and be yourself. Think of this step as an opportunity to study yourself more. Recall all the gifts, tools, and strengths you have amassed through your life experiences, some of which you may have focused on or developed more while you were reading this book.

    Then add in tangible, factually accurate information about you, including your lived experiences, strengths, career, family life, education, hobbies, and more. It's all part of the real you.

2. **Gratitude:** Next, add gratitude. You took a close look at gratitude in the Apply and Act sections of Chapter 5. It's time for another gratitude session now.

    Pause. Think about all the people, places, and things you are grateful for in your world. Smile and savor all your gratitude jewels. Add all that gratitude to What Is Real.

    Remember to express gratitude to your inner circle (including your pets) with enthusiasm. They support the real you through your lightest and darkest days.

3. **What Is with Gratitude:** You began with What Is Real and you added Gratitude, which equals What Is with Gratitude.

    What just transpired? You elevated your thoughts to empower yourself to love your life while appreciating the real you. Tapping into the Gratitude Equation daily will allow you to focus on a life that feels good.

As a complete being with a career and a personal life, you are moving forward in the direction of your ambitions, desires, and needs. Yes, keep moving forward. Yes, there are more goals to accomplish. There's no ultimate finish line in that regard. You will still encounter days when you feel exhausted, frustrated, and like it would be a lot easier to be lazy or to accept mediocrity. However, that's not the real you. The real you is ready to see the beauty in the blessings you already hold in your life.

> **Choose to be grateful for your life.
> Choose what success means to you.**

It's time to really live your life. Choose to find love for your life. Choose to find listening to yourself. If you don't take the time to find what you deeply appreciate in your life, you may be forever chasing definitions of success created by others. Choosing to find the real you means you create a definition of success for you—and empower yourself to achieve it.

Choose to be grateful for your life. Choose what success means to you.

## Act: Gratitude Goals

One actionable way to hold yourself accountable for loving your life and defining success is to embed gratitude in your daily life. Think of this next exercise as a complement to the Gratitude Equation.

As a business owner, you are well-acquainted with formulating and achieving goals. Your personal and professional goals can be synchronous. You also know that goals are "supposed" to be specific, measurable, achievable, relevant, and time-bound. For the purposes of this exercise, I'm offering you a shortcut to achieving your gratitude goals because there is no reason to make feeling gratitude and loving your life more complicated.

Overall, your specific, viable goal is to practice gratitude every day (which makes it time-bound). It is also achievable, measurable, and relevant.

Here's how to use gratitude goals to get re-inspired about your life. Ask yourself these four questions daily, as many times as you want:

1. Did I express gratitude today? (yes or no)
2. Did I express appreciation to my inner circle, colleagues, acquaintances, or anyone else today? (yes or no)
3. What are at least five things (big or small) I am most grateful for right now? (list five)
4. Do I feel better about myself and my life after this practice of gratitude? (yes or no)

Use this opportunity to tune into any little pleasure you may not currently be appreciating in your fast-paced life. For example, enjoy hearing a favorite song, listening to the rain, whipping up a home-cooked meal from a new recipe, laughing with a friend, or any other small thing that boosts your day.

If you're having a tough day, be open to doing the exercise anyway. It will help you see that no matter what is swirling in your life, there is no need to downsize your goals or to settle for less. Overall, it puts the ups, downs, and in-betweens of life in perspective.

Your life can feel good and be loved by the real you. Make it happen with maximum effort. LTY.

*Remember, put your best effort into appreciating the real you so you can love and live your best, most successful life. And smile while being kind.*

## Ask

1. While reading this chapter, did you think of something you've put on hold in your life?
2. After reading this chapter, is there something you want to commit to do? What is it? How will you make it happen for yourself?

## SOLIDIFY WHAT YOU'VE LEARNED

◊ **LESSON 1:** Change course when a new path feels right.

◊ **LESSON 2:** Collect skills and confidence.

◊ **LESSON 3:** Let the strength of kindness flow through you.

◊ **LESSON 4:** Stay driven in the moment to excel under pressure.

◊ **LESSON 5:** Persevere with gratitude.

◊ **LESSON 6:** Redefine what accessibility means to you.

◊ **LESSON 7:** Choose to show up as the real you.

◊ **LESSON 8:** Trust yourself.

◊ **LESSON 9:** Cherish your inner circle.

◊ **LESSON 10:** Stop overthinking and get going.

◊ **LESSON 11:** Get strategic about your time.

◊ **LESSON 12:** Do what matters most and delegate the rest.

◊ **LESSON 13:** Love your life.

## CONCLUSION
# A FOUNDER CHOOSES WHAT SUCCESS MEANS

At this point, do you feel more connected with the real you, ready to trust yourself, and do what matters most?

Much of what took me decades to figure out, I shared through this book to help high-achieving business owners like you reduce your stress, increase your fulfillment, and discover unique treasures that no one can take away from you. Your new portfolio includes:

- Thirteen shining diamonds (lessons).
- Vital LTY tool.
- Simplifying ALD approach.
- Space-creating Silence Solution.
- Recentering Gratitude Equation.

> **Stand tall in your self-created sunshine as the more relaxed, confident, and empowered real you.**

Your days of limiting your own progress are behind you. Stand tall in your self-created sunshine as the more relaxed, confident, and empowered real you, appreciating *all* the life experiences ahead for you.

Let's recap where you and I traveled together to collect your treasures, as you gear up to continue to work for what you want so you can truly love your life:

1. Find where you belong, so you can change course when a new path feels right.
2. Conquer opportunities to collect skills and confidence.
3. Optimize your performance and let the strength of kindness flow through you.
4. Focus to win so you can excel under pressure.
5. Carve out space to persevere with gratitude.
6. Learn to chill so you can redefine what accessibility means to you.
7. Look inside and choose to show up as the real you.
8. Feel your emotions and trust yourself.
9. Shift your perspective to cherish your inner circle.
10. Renew your energy so you can stop overthinking and get going.
11. Be your catalyst for change and get strategic about your time.
12. Stop trying to do it all so you can do what matters and delegate the rest.
13. Appreciate the real you so you can love your life.

As you have experienced, a self-aware and self-assured founder chooses what they find. You are the catalyst for the changes you want to experience. The marvelous beauty of business ownership is that there is always more to accomplish, along with unbridled ways to create, grow, and advance.

Choosing to live life as the real you is the key to owning yourself and the life you choose to live. There is no external magic that will create the success you want. You create the magic through your continued commitment to integrate your experiences, progress forward, and keep executing. Keep in mind that sometimes you're more ready than you think to take a road you haven't stepped on yet and see how far you go and where you lead yourself.

## A FOUNDER CHOOSES WHAT SUCCESS MEANS

*What opportunity will you conquer next?*

Use the perspectives, lessons, and tools I shared in this book as your strategic advantage to align your business with the real you. Connect with yourself, create what matters most, and define your success. LTY.

Thank you for entrusting me as your strategic guide. Keep creating the magnificent life you want for yourself. And remember, you're not alone.

I'd love to hear how this book helped you. Feel free to contact me with your stories, questions, or insights at JenniferMusser@JLMAConsulting.com.

As you continue your personal entrepreneurial adventure, I am here to support you. Visit JLMAConsulting.com to connect. I've also included a Discussion Guide, Workbook Exercises, and Further Resources at the end of this book.

Together we can align our businesses to connect with each other, cocreate what matters most, and make success happen.

Until we meet again,

*Jennifer*

# FURTHER RESOURCES

Start getting results right now. Continue to Align Your Business with the Real You to Connect with Yourself, Create What Matters Most, and Define Your Success.

Join our community and let me help empower you with financial and operational tools to support growth:

1. **Subscribe to our email list** to receive valuable news, business insights, and special offers to boost your business. Visit JLMAConsulting.com, go to the bottom of any page, and sign up.
2. **Arrange one-time services or ongoing support** to fit your objectives for a personalized and guided approach. Visit JLMAConsulting.com/ContactUs page and complete the form to inquire.
3. **Renew your business through our transformative Small Business Progression Program experience**, customized to your strategic goals. Learn more at JLMAConsulting.com/SmallBusinessProgessionProgram.
4. **Arrange customized Align Your Business with the Real You workshops, training, keynotes, panel discussions, and more** by contacting Jennifer directly at JenniferMusser@JLMAConsulting.com.

5. Use the **Discussion Guide and Workbook Exercises** as additional resources for you within this book.

   Find out more at JLMAConsulting.com.

   If you have any other questions, email Info@JLMAConsulting or call 1-888-332-0045.

# DISCUSSION GUIDE

This guide is a compilation of all the Ask reflection questions so you have them in one place for your convenience. This is also a useful guide for book club discussions.

## Chapter 1: Find Where You Belong

1. Think of a time when you had to make a profound pivot. How did you recognize that a change in course would suit you better? How did you feel before, during, and after this pivot?
2. What does "find where you belong" mean to you in the context of your career and life?

## Chapter 2: Conquer Opportunities

1. Think of one unexpected life experience that enabled you to collect useful skills and valuable confidence. How does that noteworthy experience benefit you today?

2. What is one heavy thing you want to unload right now from your figurative suitcase? Is there anything holding you back from offloading it?
3. How will you take action to listen to yourself (LTY) more?

## Chapter 3: Optimize Your Performance

1. How has the concept "kindness is strong" shown up in your life? In your business?
2. Where do you like to go to reset your mind for a few minutes, hours, or days?

## Chapter 4: Focus to Win

1. What distracts you most from staying driven to focus on your wins?
2. What can you do for yourself today to dial down the external and internal noise?

## Chapter 5: Carve Out Space

1. Name one significant challenge you're currently facing that you must persevere through.
2. Think back to the direst event you had to persevere through in the past. How did you make it through? What strengths were revealed? How were you changed for the better?
3. How might your strengths and lessons from your experience help you in your current challenge?

## Chapter 6: Learn to Chill

1. Can you think of a time in your life when you lost something significant, and that loss created space for something more fulfilling? Did you set this change in motion, or was it decided for you?
2. Before you read this chapter, what did accessibility mean to you? Now what does it mean? Did your view of accessibility change? If so, how?

## Chapter 7: Look Inside

1. Can you think of a time in your life when a passing moment led to a lasting, beneficial outcome for you? How did the outcome unfold for you?
2. Before you read this chapter, what did "showing up as the real you" mean to you? Now what does it mean to you? What did you learn that will impact the way you show up?

## Chapter 8: Feel Your Emotions

1. Have you ever experienced a loss that resulted in you feeling stuck? How did you get unstuck?
2. Before you read this chapter, did you trust yourself to seek and receive guidance when you needed it? What insight or action will you put into practice to help you trust yourself?

## Chapter 9: Shift Your Perspective

1. Has a notable life experience ever caused you to shift your perspective? What happened? How did the experience change your perspective?

2. Before you read this chapter, did you regularly nurture your inner circle? What will you do starting now to further cherish these important relationships in your life?

## Chapter 10: Renew Your Energy

1. Do you recall a time when you felt renewed energy? What triggered it? What changes did you experience before or after your energy boost?
2. How do you prevent yourself from overthinking?
3. Will you use different language after reading this chapter? How will you begin?

## Chapter 11: Be Your Catalyst for Change

1. Are you aware when you are wasting your time? What is your biggest time suck? How do you prevent yourself from wasting time?
2. After reading this chapter, how will you get more strategic about your time?

## Chapter 12: Stop Trying to Do It All

1. Do you view delegation as an obstacle? Or do you delegate well? Do you follow through and follow up?
2. After reading this chapter, how will you pare down your workload to start doing what matters most? What will you delegate within the next sixty days?

## Chapter 13: Appreciate the Real You

1. While reading this chapter, did you think of something you've put on hold in your life?
2. After reading this chapter, is there something you want to commit to do? What is it? How will you make it happen for yourself?

# WORKBOOK EXERCISES

This book was designed so you could learn your way. Some prefer to do each exercise as they read, while others prefer to learn the concepts as a whole first and then return to the exercises later.

For those who prefer to focus on their practical application, here is a mini-workbook with all the exercises from each chapter in one place to complete on your own schedule.

## Chapter 1: Find Where You Belong

### Lesson 1: Change course when a new path feels right.
### Act: Then, Now, Next

Here is an exercise to try as your next step. (Remember, all the exercises also appear at the end of the book for your convenience. If you'd prefer to keep reading and complete the exercises later, please do. This book was designed to offer you flexibility, so use it to your advantage.)

If you think you might need to change course, consider the following questions:

1. **Then:** Think back to recall how many times you have pivoted since the "green" phase of your early twenties. How did you know you needed to make a change? Any answer is a good one here, as it will help you recognize similar circumstances now.
2. **Now:** Shift your focus to your current situation. In your current work life, what makes you whirl in circles? We're not talking about tasks you'd rather not deal with, like bookkeeping or tax planning (we'll deal with delegation later); think of situations where you feel as if you're unable to move forward. We're often trying to avoid some inner discomfort, or we don't have the strategic expertise to know how to move forward. In either case, we don't resolve the issue.
3. **Next:** Now that you've uncovered what makes you swirl, how do you stop it? Remember your commitment to act with intention and strategic speed. Use what you know about yourself and your business to get on the most suitable success path. For example, if marketing to your target audience is falling flat, it's time to adjust. If your business model is the source of your angst, lead yourself to the root cause. Be honest with yourself.

If you can't solve it alone, tap into your connections to seek advice or hire expert guidance within your budget. Chapter 12 dives further into this topic. For now, keep in mind that the longer you delay, the more you are exacerbating your business issue.

## Chapter 2: Conquer Opportunities

### Lesson 2: Collect skills and confidence.
### Act: Unpack, Repack, Repeat

In this exercise, you will unpack and repack your figurative suitcase containing all your professional experiences so you can keep the skills and confidence you've built and let go of all that weighs you down.

# WORKBOOK EXERCISES

1. **Unpack:** Imagine you're unloading the luggage from all your travels—in the form of professional experiences up to this point in your life. What have you been carrying? Make a list of your useful skills, the unique abilities that set you apart, and the unnecessary stuff that weighs you down.

    Your useful and unique skills are a big part of the reason you are a capable business owner. Useful skills are your core abilities that help you lead your business. Unique skills are your differentiating factors. These attract your ideal customers and colleagues to you, setting you apart from competitors.

    Unnecessary baggage is the heavy stuff you carry around in your mind that stifles your development. Here is your chance to unload.

    Let's unpack. Examples are included below to get you started.

    | Useful | Unique | Unnecessary |
    | --- | --- | --- |
    | Time management | Listening with eyes | What-ifs |
    | Collaborative attitude | Mental stamina | Self-judgment |
    |  |  |  |

2. **Pack:** Now pack your bag with the useful and unique skills you want to take with you on your next collection journey. This time, you are replacing unnecessary baggage with focused desires. You are deciding what you seek as you embrace more opportunities to grow you and your business.

    The purpose of this part of the exercise is to illustrate that you have much of what you need to acquire more abilities. (I packed LTY for you on this next trip.)

    You are lightening your load by focusing on what you need to embrace, do, and collect.

| Useful | Unique | Focused Desires |
|---|---|---|
| Time management | Listening with eyes | Write a book |
| Collaborative attitude | Mental stamina | Launch a new service |
| LTY | Writing | Collaborate with another entrepreneur |
|  |  |  |

3. **Repeat:** Going forward, you can repeat this process after each new opportunity. As you acquire more and more knowledge, your useful and unique lists will grow. Meanwhile, your focused desires might change as you elevate yourself to conquer more opportunities.

| Useful | Unique | Focused Desires |
|---|---|---|
|  |  |  |
|  |  |  |
|  |  |  |
|  |  |  |

## Chapter 3: Optimize Your Performance

### Lesson 3: Let the strength of kindness flow through you. Act: Assemble Your Strengths Toolkit

You are now prepared to start assembling your toolkit in two steps:

1. **Identify your strategic strengths.** As you assemble your strengths toolkit, keep in mind that strategic strengths aren't confined to the work world. For business owners, career and personal lives blend.

    Some useful and unique skills that you identified in Chapter 2's exercise may reappear in your strengths column. This exercise is intended to go deeper. Focus on your strengths that give you differentiating competitive advantages as a business owner.

Remember, you don't need to excel at everything in all facets of your business and life. Be honest with yourself. Some strengths you need to elevate your business you can fill in through strategic delegation. We'll talk more about delegation in Chapter 12.

Also, by this point, you may have started to develop your skill of LTY. So you may want to list LTY as one of your strengths or commit to transforming LTY to a strength. Try to not over index on strategic strengths. Bullets and not run on sentences are the goal.

| Identify Strategic Strengths |
| --- |
| Crafting unique offerings |
| Exploring value opportunities |
| Solving problems |
| Personalizing solutions |
| Leading with kindness |
| Expressing courtesies |
| Utilizing mental stamina |
| LTY |

2. **Choose how kindness flows in your business.** Kindness enables you to work stronger, more connected with yourself and others. Your capacity for kindness is an excellent diagnostic and a sign of working in alignment with your strengths. Where does kindness flow in your business? Are you tapping into kindness as a strength? How are you demonstrating kindness?

Let's begin. Examples are included below to help get you started.

| **Make Kindness a Strategic Strength** |
| --- |
| Saying consistently please and thank you (and meaning it) |
| Expressing gratitude toward clients |
| Showing appreciation for your team—and caring for them |
| Adding levity to the workday |
| Expressing interest in your clients' and team members' work |
| Respecting others' time (don't schedule meetings at 3 p.m. on a Friday in the summer) |
| Being generous within your means—it's not all about you |
| Giving to others in alignment with the real you |

## Chapter 4: Focus to Win

### Lesson 4: Stay driven in the moment to excel under pressure.
### Act: Visualize the Win

At this point, you are ready to spot and reduce distractions to reduce noise in your life. You want to win consistently. With more focused effort, you will.

1. **Assess your distractions.** Recognize that you don't have control over all the distractions that may arise, so you can't prevent all of them from occurring. However, you can identify your biggest problem areas to help yourself.

   In the boxes below, rank your performance distractions from one to four, with one being the top distraction and four being the lowest.

   For example, unintentional internal distractions may be your biggest barriers if your mind tends to fire on all cylinders at all times. Intentional internal distractions may be third if you've learned to limit your intentional distractions. Unintentional external distractions may be second, if that's how you feel your life's been lately.

# WORKBOOK EXERCISES

If you have mastered the skill of not caring what others do or say to you or about you, intentional external distractions may be your lowest with a number four in that box. (On the contrary, if that stuff gets you off-kilter, you might rank it as one.)

## Performance Distractions

| Rank 1–4<br>1 Top Distraction,<br>4 Lowest | Intentional | Unintentional |
| --- | --- | --- |
| External | | |
| Internal | | |

2. **Customize your training.** Your top two ranked categories are where you need to train. You need to develop your customized practice routine for focus so you can apply it when it counts.

    For example, if external categories are more distracting for you, train here to get stronger. If internal categories rank higher because you tend to interrupt yourself more often than others distract you, then that's where you need to devote effort.

    This is where visualization will serve as your personal trainer. Let's get started.

3. **Visualize your win.** Visualization can help you prepare to excel.

    First, you are going to recall a bad business experience. Think about a super tough day, a lost bid for new work, a poorly done presentation, whatever jumps into your mind. (There's a reason for this—keep reading.)

    Now think about *why* it went the way it did. Be totally honest with yourself. No one is listening. And refrain from the blame game. Were you super stressed? What was distracting you? Were you going through the motions? Was your mind not in the game? Did you not treat someone well? Did you not quality control your work product? Did you lack sleep? You'll know the answer.

    Then let it go.

    Next, combine your insights from that experience with your

findings from the first part of this exercise to focus on your next win. Close your eyes. Imagine your top two ranked distractors are gone. What does winning feel like now? Is it easier? Are you more driven? Are you more present in the moment? Are you excelling? Does the pressure feel lessened? If you're visualizing your next win, the answer to all these questions is *yes*.

Why? Because now you are planning ahead, communicating what you want, limiting involvement with external distractions, ignoring what isn't important, and focusing with all your might on what does matter. You and your business matter. Go for the win.

# Chapter 5: Carve Out Space

## Lesson 5: Persevere with gratitude.
## Act: The Gratitude Equation

When you're navigating a challenging long-term life event like a health issue or major challenge, it takes dedicated effort and energy to pull yourself through. You can carve out space for yourself to accept what is and free yourself from the unproductive thoughts in your mind. Then you can focus on being grateful for what matters most.

This is no small feat. To accomplish it, here is a tool I call the Gratitude Equation:

**The Gratitude Equation**™

$$\textit{What Is Real} - \textit{What Is Not Real} + \textit{Gratitude} = \textit{What Is with Gratitude}$$

## WORKBOOK EXERCISES

Here are the four steps:

1. **What Is Real:** For this exercise, What Is Real includes what you know to be true about what you are going through. For example, it includes what your pathology report actually says in writing, what your doctor told you directly, or your lab work results. In other words, this is tangible, factually accurate information.
2. **What Is Not Real:** Then subtract What Is Not Real from What Is Real. What Is Not Real (you see it disappearing above) encompasses the countless and torturous scenarios you play in your mind, such as all your doom and gloom, worst-case scenarios, what you imagine others are thinking or saying about your situation, and more. Acknowledge them all, and then let them go. You are removing them from your Gratitude Equation.
3. **Gratitude:** Next, add gratitude. List all the things that are right in your world, as you may have already done in Apply: Step 4. Whatever you are grateful for, feel it, think it, and hold on to it. Imagine you are holding your gratitude jewels in your hands. You want to hold so many that they are spilling over.

    For instance, your gratitude jewels may include your most enjoyable vacation memory, the taste of your favorite food, the sound of your loved one's laughter, an image of playtime with your pets, the scenic sight of a still, blue ocean or white snow-capped mountains, and so on. Envision all the folks who add value to your life because they make you feel good. For example, you may be grateful that your or your loved one's diagnosis was caught early or turned out to be the better-case scenario. You can be grateful for little things like the delicious pancakes you ate at a diner yesterday with your friend. There is no right or wrong answer. Add all that gratitude to What Is Real.
4. **What Is with Gratitude:** You have now taken control of your thoughts about your tough situation. You began with What Is Real, you eliminated What Is Not Real, and you added Gratitude, which equals What Is with Gratitude. You elevated your thoughts to empower yourself to persevere with gratitude.

Recall the Gratitude Equation in your mind whenever you are thrown a curveball you weren't expecting. LTY. The first sign you need to use your Gratitude Equation is when your mind starts wandering into What Is Not Real territory. When this happens, carve out space for yourself to focus on What Is with Gratitude.

## Chapter 6: Learn to Chill

### Lesson 6: Redefine what accessibility means to you. Act: The Silence Solution

As you redefine your accessibility, you can use what I call the Silence Solution as a tool to preserve your personal space as needed. The Silence Solution will enhance your chill time.

Here are the two simple steps to find peace in silence:

1. **Adjust your calendar.** First, prioritize regular time to be *alone* in silence. This is not the time to work out, do work, read email, or check social media. This is time you will spend with yourself in silence. For example, you can meditate, take a walk outside, or sit alone (pets are allowed) to gather your thoughts for the day.

   When would you most benefit from this time? Is it first thing in the morning before your house wakes up? Is it mid-afternoon when you start to feel the work pile on? Is it before the dinner time chaos? Is it at night, right before you drift off to sleep? If spending time in silence is not part of your regular practice, start with at least one optimal time slot for an increment of at least ten minutes twice per week. *Yes, you can.*

   Next, block out the time on your calendar and set an alarm on your phone to hold you accountable. Play around with the time slots and length of time. When you find ones that work, build up to five days per week, then daily. Give the results time to kick in. Once you feel your daily mood and energy improve, you will want to commit

to your chill time. You will start to crave it. Ask me how I know.
2. **Adjust your reaction to others.** For this one, think about the most recent infringements on your personal space. For example, it might be the person who constantly wants from you, the filterless person who asks you nosy questions, the terse text message you received from someone who didn't have the temerity to pick up the phone, or the so-called friend or colleague who bad mouths you when you're not around (but they act nice to your face). The specific list of unnecessary energy-zapping exchanges will be unique for every individual, but we all have them.

    None of them matter. You are in control of how you respond to each and every occurrence. And you can choose to respond in silence. A snippy text message doesn't earn a response. You don't owe nosy types answers about your life to give them fresh material for their gossip cliques. Those who talk badly behind your back don't get any more of your time or energy. No, no, and no. Sometimes, silence is the best and only answer.

Use this two-part Silence Solution whenever you need to create space for yourself or establish a limit. LTY. Repeat the steps as often as needed. Tweak as you go. Let silence be part of your solution to stress.

The Silence Solution may leave a few folks perplexed. That's okay. As long as you apply these strategies with kindness, you aren't doing anything wrong. In fact, your silence is speaking volumes about how you're owning what is yours, including your respect and self-worth.

# Chapter 7: Look Inside

## Lesson 7: Choose to show up as the real you.
## Act: The Five-Layer Cake

After completing the four Apply steps to help you choose to show up as the real you, you are ready to bring the real you to wherever you are. To do so, you can share the "Five-Layer Cake," created, mixed, baked, and assembled to perfection by you. The five layers represent aspects of yourself that you want to share with the world. Private aspects of your life that you don't intend to share are not baked into the cake.

You get to choose how you will craft your cake combination. No shopping, oven, or calories required. Be creative as you compile all the layers of the real you.

Here are the five layers from bottom to top:

- **Layer 1: Who.** Who do you enjoy spending time with? (Pets count.) Who makes you feel valued? Who makes you feel happiest?

  The "who" comes first because these are the ones you want to be sure to share your cake with and spend more time with.
- **Layer 2: What.** What do you do for work? What do you do for fun? What topics do you like talking about? What are your hobbies and interests? What music do you listen to? What sports do you follow?

What shows do you watch? What books do you read? What makes you laugh?

Share these things with others at a meeting, event, dinner, or other public setting.
- **Layer 3: When.** When do you feel your best? When do you do your clearest thinking? When do you look your best? When do you smile most?

    This layer helps you show up clear minded, engaged, and looking and feeling fabulous.
- **Layer 4: Where.** Where are your favorite spots to think, work, play, dine, rest? Where do you like to go for fun? Where do you go to relax? Where do you feel the most comfortable?

    Frequent these places more. It's easier to walk in a room smiling and shining when you are where you want to be.
- **Layer 5: How.** How are you unique? How do you want to project the real you? How do you bring kindness as a strength? How much do you smile and laugh during your workday? How do you chill?

    Visualize the inner you shining through the outer you. Bring the you that radiates your good vibes to others.
- **Icing, Sprinkles, and a Cherry on Top: Personality.** What's your style? How do you show up externally? What comprises the external layer of your personality that others see?

    When you bring your cake to a party, this is what others see first. As you put the finishing touches on your cake, think of the icing as the fashion styles and colors you choose. Sprinkles symbolize your ability to add levity, laughter, and love to any room. Finally, the cherry on top is the smile that speaks volumes in any room, in any situation.

Keep in mind that the Five-Layer Cake you bake today may not be the same cake you make six months or a year or three years from now. The flavors of your layers may change as you evolve. For example, your "What" layer could change as your business morphs into something else or your interests or tastes shift. That's all okay.

Repeat this exercise as often as you want to bake new cakes that reflect the current version of you.

## Chapter 8: Feel Your Emotions

### Lesson 8: Trust yourself.
### Act: The Sandcastle

To help you trust yourself and your inner guidance to create a new phase in your life, this exercise will reconnect you with the natural trust in yourself you had as a child whenever you created something new. For this exercise, you are going to tap into your creativity to build an *imaginary* sandcastle.

Imaginary? Yes, I know you are a professional adult. Trust me; flow with it.

Imagine yourself as a child visiting the beach, seeing the expanse of sand and waves before you. All you can think about is building a sandcastle. This sandcastle is envisioned by you. Built by you. Molded by you with your bare hands.

No two sandcastles are the same. There are different formations, heights, widths. Elaborate works of sandcastle art can enter the realm of sculpture. Similar to building a business, when building a sandcastle, there is no limit to your vision.

For the purposes of this imaginary project, you aren't using your left brain. Don't research what beaches have the best sand, calculate the perfect sand-to-water ratio, or use fancy tools.

This is an exercise in using your creative mind. You are building this sandcastle yourself without co-creation or collaboration because this is an exercise in trusting yourself.

Here's what you need:

- **Tool:** LTY. You are listening to yourself about what, when, where, and how to build what you want to construct. Let your imaginary hands go where your mind takes you.

  Also, you're not asking someone for advice, input, or approval. You're working independently while trusting yourself.
- **Materials:** Your imagination plus imaginary water and sand are all you need.

  Envision your sandcastle in your mind's eye and use your imagination to build it now.

  As you "work" with nature, keep in mind that you can't force it. If your proportion of water and sand aren't quite right, you won't be able to create the intended structure, no matter how hard you try. Too much water, the sand won't mold. With too little water, the formation will crumble.

  At this point, you may be wondering, *Why am I doing this? What is really going on here?* You trust that you can use what you've got to build what you set out to build. You are tapping into your creativity, independence, and will to succeed. Think of the sandcastle as a phase of life you are envisioning and building for yourself.
- **Attitude:** Patience is the most useful attitude here. It's okay if you don't get the right mix the first time. Make an adjustment, try again, and you'll get it.

  You know from building sandcastles as a kid or with your family members that you can't rush it. It takes time and patience. Think slow and steady.

Admire the beautiful sandcastle molded with your own hands, imagination, and patience in your mind. You created it.

No matter how many barriers you craft to protect your castle, a wave will come and wash it away. Don't spend time building barriers. Instead, revel in the fact that you created something beautiful on your own. Most importantly, now you trust yourself to know what to do to rebuild it.

Now that you've reconnected with the trust and creativity you've always had within you, what phase of your life will you build next?

## Chapter 9: Shift Your Perspective

### Lesson 9: Cherish your inner circle.
### Act: Cherish Rings

To help you appreciate the relationships that truly matter, in this wellness exercise you will focus on the qualities of individuals you consider part of your inner circle.

In five steps, you're going to examine, visualize, and treasure each individual in your inner circle with Cherish Rings:

1. **Imagine a ring** representing each friend or family member in your inner circle. (If you prefer to draw these rings with paper and pen, then do so, although it's not necessary.)

    Feel free to include a circle for your pets; after all, you comfort, love, and support each other.

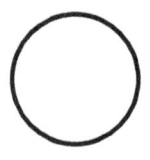

2. **Then, starting with the first individual, visualize words inside the ring that describe why you believe this person is exceptional.** Assemble a list of their attributes in your mind. For example, the first person who pops into your mind may stir up words like compassionate, accepting, trustworthy, honest, kind, generous, thoughtful, patient, sweet, and soothing. You may recall little things they do for

you or that you do together, like helping you cook, baking the best homemade cookies, or traveling with you to explore new destinations. They may have done something big for you, such as comforting you during a horrible loss or illness.

3. **Move on to the next individual, visualizing words that describe that person in a separate ring, until you have a ring for each member of your inner circle.** For example, the next person could be loving, accepting, trustworthy, honest, kind, funny, organized, disciplined, and so on. You may recall how much you laugh when you're together, how you exchange stories about all your dog's funny antics, and how you help each other navigate the phases of parenthood. You get the idea.

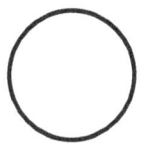

◯

After you go through this part of the exercise, you may have a handful or so of circles created. Even if you have just one or two circles filled with reasons why someone is treasured by you, you are blessed. There are no right or wrong answers, and no number is too few. As mentioned earlier, your inner circle is about quality, not quantity.

4. **Now pause.** Soak in all the positive thoughts you released into your reality. You have a thorough appreciation of the importance of the ones who contribute to your life experience. They help you see a brighter, stronger, more complete version of yourself when you look in the mirror. And you can do that for them too.

Okay, pause time is over. Moving on.

5. **Get curious about similar words within your rings.** What traits do your inner-circle members have in common?

Examine these traits more closely. Using the examples above, you might notice the words trustworthy, accepting, honest, and kind appear in both rings. No surprise. Those are inner-circle worthy traits.

Would you want deceitful, judgmental, and mean personalities close to you? No way.

```
TRUSTWORTHY
ACCEPTING
HONEST
KIND
```

These traits are likely ones you highly value or see in yourself too. Feelings of personal gratitude may be kicking in right about now. That's a good thing.

What will you do next? That's up to you. You might choose to reach out to each friend or family member you thought about during this exercise. You might choose to schedule time with them to nourish both of your souls. You get the idea.

WORKBOOK EXERCISES

# Chapter 10: Renew Your Energy

## Lesson 10: Stop overthinking and get going.
Act: Word Find

## Word Find

```
W U E T L R K A Z U P Q P D U
M K X U Z S B U B B M A Y B E
S G Q E J N H T J L E A D A G
Y H A N H U P O J A M G H A E
L N Z D I T D K U G H E T M P
F X O K Z A R J N L B Y E Y A
N R Q N P C P I S W D D W T X
X N X X B I W X L M H Q I R I
Z S Y Y Q W K V K O S A L I F
D V F H F T E S U I D C T P T
M E W P A M Q I O O S G K I C
N R V A I J Y T U S C R J C F
B F W N A V C J T K W A W Q N
X G X E X W B O V G C O N M D
T L J N B F M Y J S F O M T R
```

Should    What If    Maybe    Can't

In the Apply section, we reviewed how vocabulary, thoughts, and outcomes tie together. This Word Find exercise will help you focus on the words you *choose* to use in the life you *choose* to live. It's also for the entrepreneurs out there who love a good brain teaser.

For this word find, you aren't searching for words on paper. You're searching for these words in your daily vocabulary:

- Should
- What if
- Maybe
- Can't

Once you commit to this exercise, it becomes a game, where the only person you're competing against is yourself. Who do you want to win: the overthinking, "never enough" version of yourself or the "commit to become more, LTY more" version of yourself? Whoever you allow to declare victory is up to you.

Here's how to get going:

- **Mentally note when you say the words should, what if, maybe, and can't.** For example, recognize that you used the word should two times in the last ten minutes. Imagine how many times you say it in an entire day? You get the idea.
- **Pay attention to when you use these words and what (or whom) you're referring to.** For example, are you referring to yourself, saying things like, "I should get to bed earlier during the week"? Or are you flinging these words at your inner circle or colleagues, using expressions like, "We should meet for lunch"? (Drop the should, schedule the lunch.) Or, "What if we start the project in January"? (Tell your colleague, "I am scheduling a new project to kick off mid-January.) Or, "I can't take on your project"? (Be more straightforward: you're currently booked, their budget is too low, or their needs don't align with your services.)
- **Mind your maybes.** The word *maybe* can be useful when you're not sure if something is true and you want to offer the possibility. For example, when connecting with others in writing or a presentation, you may list several scenarios they "may" relate with, but you don't know for sure; you're offering possibilities. However, other times, the word *maybe* belongs in the trash, such as, "Maybe I'll go," when you have no intention of going. Tell the person you won't make it. Respect them by being honest.

With consistent word find practice, eventually these words won't roll off your tongue like they did before. Also, be patient with yourself. This new habit takes commitment and action. Eliminating the word *should* is the hardest.

# Chapter 11: Be Your Catalyst for Change

## Lesson 11: Get strategic about your time.
## Act: The Keystone

The unique keystone of your business is you. You must stay strong as the most important stone at the top of your arch, in this case, your life.

The keystone of your calendar is your time to work on your business without anyone else around. Keep in mind your keystone time is separate from the Silence Solution time we covered in Chapter 6, for you to you spend alone, not working, to collect your thoughts for the day. This keystone is the most important part of your weekly work schedule. If you find time to reallocate, this is the place.

Setting aside focused time alone to work on your business is an essential stamina-builder. It supports all the other moves you make that week. It supports your clarity as you choose opportunities to pursue. It supports the success of your outcomes.

This exercise will help you create a weekly calendar keystone as a first step to building your schedule and being strategic about your time. You will use your calendar keystone to do the following:

- *Think* creatively.
- *Plan* your week, month, and year. For example, in the last quarter of the year, you can block additional time to plan for the first half of the following year. Planning time is required for budgeting, business development, marketing, and creating.
- *Organize* what you need and when for clients, events, appointments, supplies, inventory, budgeting, marketing, and banking. Send follow-up emails or confirmations that require your direct involvement.

- *Create* what you planned. This could include fresh service offerings, social media posts, blogs, marketing materials, new training curriculum, event plans, presentations, or business pitches.
- *Do* the work you need to accomplish yourself, in peace and quiet. This is anything that requires you to focus, with zero interruptions.
- *Breathe.* Stay strategic by considering your new, transformed, strategic schedule you worked on in the last section.

Now set your weekly keystone.

What block of time per week will you set aside to do what only you can do for your business?

You can block out one longer session per week or two sessions per week. You choose what will work best for you, based on your personality and business. Some choose Fridays to plan for the following week. Some prefer the first day of the work week, which varies based on your business. Others prefer midweek.

As you consider where to set this weekly keystone, select times when you can have peace. Your office is quiet. Your team is not in the same place as you. Your significant other is at work. Your kids are out of the house. Your dogs are asleep. Your phone is put aside for emergency use. You get the idea.

When is your calendar keystone? Schedule this time to support the rest of your week, months, and year.

Make it happen.

| WEEKLY CALENDAR | | | | | | | |
|---|---|---|---|---|---|---|---|
| | SUN | MON | TUE | WED | THU | FRI | SAT |
| 6 am | | | | | | | |
| 7 am | | | | | | | |
| 9 am | | | | | | | |
| 10 am | | | | | | | |
| 11 am | | | | | | | |
| noon | | | | | | | |
| 1 pm | | | | | | | |
| 2 pm | | | | | | | |
| 3 pm | | | | | | | |
| 4 pm | | | | | | | |
| 5 pm | | | | | | | |
| 6 pm | | | | | | | |
| 7 pm | | | | | | | |
| 8 pm | | | | | | | |
| 9 pm | | | | | | | |
| 10 pm | | | | | | | |

Then play around with your new calendar. Test it out. Make necessary adjustments. Stick with it for sustainable transformation.

You're creating lasting change for yourself, which is a challenging feat filled with opportunity.

# Chapter 12: Stop Trying to Do It All

## Lesson 12: Do what matters most and delegate the rest.
## Act: If/Then

In the Chapter 2 exercise, you worked on "unpacking" the "what ifs" weighing you down. Then, in Chapter 10, you started to eliminate "what if" from your vocabulary as part of your effort to stop overthinking and get going.

Now, we are going to use "if" combined with "then" in a useful way to illustrate the cause-and-effect relationship between delegation and results.

The key assumptions are:

- Tasks delegated are within the monthly budget without incurring debt.
- Execution can occur within the sixty-day deadline mentioned in the section above.
- All the delegated activities save you time, which enables you to accomplish more of what you want.

To ensure you can delegate while staying within your monthly budget, start identifying ways you can save money and redirect it to outsourcing the work that makes the most sense for you to delegate. For example, saving a couple hundred dollars a month can help you offload a task, even if it's relatively small. Think of it this way: If I cancel the XYZ service that costs me $150 per month—that I'm not even using—I can put that cash toward paying for [fill in the blank]. Money savings that seem small at the time can elevate your daily life in significant ways. Redirect your flow.

Here are some examples:

# WORKBOOK EXERCISES

| Life Area | If I Delegate This | Then I Can Do This |
|---|---|---|
| Work | Bookkeeping | Focus on work I love |
| Work | Strategic staffing analysis with revised budget and recommended action steps | Achieve the staffing schedule I want, a more cohesive team, and increased profit |
| Work | Front desk reception, including answering phones | Spend more time on paying clients, which will increase my bottom line |
| Personal | House cleaning | Be happier and more engaged on the weekends with my friends and family |
| Personal | Closet organization | Feel more organized, which renews my energy |

Now it's your turn. Complete the chart below based on the examples above and what you learned in this chapter. Then, determine how you can use this methodology to boost your desire to delegate and your ability to fully execute whatever you delegate.

What will you accomplish next?

| Life Area | If I Delegate This | Then I Can Do This |
|---|---|---|
| | | |
| | | |
| | | |
| | | |

# Chapter 13: Appreciate the Real You

## Lesson 13: Love your life.
## Act: Gratitude Goals

One actionable way to hold yourself accountable for loving your life and defining success is to embed gratitude in your daily life. Think of this next exercise as a complement to the Gratitude Equation.

As a business owner, you are well-acquainted with formulating and achieving goals. Your personal and professional goals can be synchronous. You also know that goals are "supposed" to be specific, measurable, achievable, relevant, and time-bound. For the purposes of this exercise, I'm offering you a shortcut to achieving your gratitude goals because there is no reason to make feeling gratitude and loving your life more complicated.

Overall, your specific, viable goal is to practice gratitude every day (which makes it time-bound). It is also achievable, measurable, and relevant.

Here's how to use gratitude goals to get re-inspired about your life. Ask yourself these four questions daily, as many times as you want:

1. Did I express gratitude today? (yes or no)
2. Did I express appreciation to my inner circle, colleagues, acquaintances, or anyone else today? (yes or no)
3. What are at least five things (big or small) I am most grateful for right now? (list five)
4. Do I feel better about myself and my life after this practice of gratitude? (yes or no)

Use this opportunity to tune into any little pleasure you may not currently be appreciating in your fast-paced life. For example, enjoy hearing a favorite song, listening to the rain, whipping up a home-cooked meal from a new recipe, laughing with a friend, or any other small thing that boosts your day.

If you're having a tough day, be open to doing the exercise anyway. It will help you see that no matter what is swirling in your life, there is no need to downsize your goals or to settle for less. Overall, it puts the ups, downs, and in-betweens of life in perspective.

Your life can feel good and be loved by the real you. Make it happen with maximum effort. LTY.

# ACKNOWLEDGMENTS AND GRATITUDE

This book was brought into the world through the support and guidance of special ones who have had a profound impact on my life and hold a special place in my heart.

To my husband, Mark, thank you for being my loving partner in life, creating a meaningful journey, and executing our visions. I cherish how we always believe in each other. You've embraced my goals, passions, and career; you embrace the real me. I love you.

Richard, you are our greatest gift, joy, and blessing. Thank you for your kind words and acts of unwavering encouragement during my author journey. You are a remarkable person. Keep shining your light, strength, and kindness in the world. I love you.

You both are a huge part of what's written on the pages of this book and in the behind-the-scenes reality. You understood the tremendous time, space, effort, and energy I devoted to bringing this book together and launching it into the world. You supported me every single step of the way. Thanks for keeping Penny and Rockie occupied when I felt inspired to write and they felt inspired to play. I love you both forever and ever.

Mom and Dad, you provided a warm, solid, love-filled home and endless encouragement, commitment, hugs, and kisses. Your willingness to read to me for hours, take me to the library for hours, and put books in my family room toy basket and on my bedroom bookshelves so I could read for hours created an avid reader who became an author. Most importantly, you taught me to be a lifelong learner, laugh for no reason, listen to music, work hard, love harder, and be kind. Thank you for being wonderful parents and extraordinary grandparents. I will be forever grateful. I love you both so much.

Grandma Ann, you will always be a beacon of light to me. Thank you for your never-ending love, devoted support, and warmth. I often felt like you were an angel on my shoulder while I was writing this book. You are part of the real me.

Roxy, Rockie, and Penny, to some, you are dogs. To our family, you are unconditional love, loyalty, and laughter, helping us stay present and focusing on what matters most. Thank you for the long walks, comfy cuddles, playtime, and for being my constant companions for every minute, every word I wrote in this book.

My talented editor, Amanda Rooker, I felt your warm heart-centered guidance from our first meeting. Thank you for encouraging me to dig into my voice, visions, and vulnerability. Through this writing journey, you became so much more than an editor to me; you are a true collaborator, confidant, and friend.

My Inner Circle, thank you for laughing, loving, and living life with me.

Barbara Misrendino, your combination of kindness, awareness, intelligence, loyalty, and support is wonderful—thank you. I am grateful we are part of each other's journey, pink peonies and all.

Susie Mann, I am grateful our kindred spirits connected. Your photography captures the real me in a fun, engaging way—thank you.

Edna Patton, thank you for being a kind, sensational, and special teacher. You helped plant seeds that eventually grew me into an author.

## ACKNOWLEDGMENTS AND GRATITUDE

Dr. Gerard Olson, thank you for welcoming me into Bartley Hall and helping me pivot from veterinary dreams into the business world where I belonged. You are an exceptional professor, advisor, and kind person who taught me about what matters most.

Cortney Donelson, thank you for adding your voice and stories to the Enlightened Leadership Blog. I appreciate your reliable, enthusiastic attention to detail.

Hannah Linder, thank you for seamlessly executing my vision for this book cover (and helping me integrate the perfect pink sky). Your creative and kind spirit got me from our first email.

David Wogahn, thank you for being an honest, knowledgeable voice, guiding me through my publication process. I am grateful we connected at the right "meant to be" time.

Manon Wogahn, I enjoy working with you. Thank you for caring for my work and helping me launch this special project in a way that aligns with the real me.

Thank you to my readers, clients, and colleagues; your support and engagement inspires me to empower as many business owners as possible.

And to all those finding where you belong, you will. LTY. To all those feeling like you want and need more, you can construct the life you envision for yourself and with others. To all those craving change, you can transform your experience. Make it happen.

With gratitude,

*Jennifer*

# ABOUT THE AUTHOR

**JENNIFER MUSSER** is the founder of JLM & Associates Consulting, LLC, where she uses her big company expertise to empower high-achieving business leaders with financial and operational tools to support growth with less stress. With a Bachelor's Degree in Business Administration (Finance) from Villanova University, Lean Six Sigma Green Belt certification, and multiple certifications in business strategy, Jennifer's passion is helping small businesses succeed. She loves life with her husband Mark, son Richard, and two dogs, Penny and Rockie, in New Jersey.

Website: JLMAConsulting.com
Instagram: @jlmaconsulting
LinkedIn: Linkedin.com/in/JenniferLMusser
Email: JenniferMusser@JLMAConsulting.com

Printed in the USA
CPSIA information can be obtained
at www.ICGtesting.com
CBHW030326011224
18182CB00005B/24